MONEY MATTERS

R.C. SPROUL, JR.

Tyndale House Publishers, Inc. Wheaton, Illinois

First printing, December 1985

Library of Congress Catalog Card Number 85-51497
ISBN 0-8423-4540-X
Copyright 1985 by R. C. Sproul, Jr.
Printed in the United States of America

To Mr. and Mrs. Robert D. Love,
servants of God and of freedom

In loving memory of William Raymond Voorhis,
a man who knew the value of hard work

CONTENTS

FOREWORD

I stared at the television set in stunned disbelief. The hour was late and I thought perhaps I had dozed off and was experiencing a nightmare. I focused my eyes and strained my ears as the announcement confirmed the stark reality. Bobby Kennedy had just been shot at close range. Pictures of Rosie Grier wrestling with the assailant brought the ugly truth home.

In 1968 I was a theological conservative and a political liberal. I was actively campaigning for Robert Kennedy's bid for the Democratic nomination for the office of president of the United States. His assassination smashed my hopes to ruins. In the 1972 election I wrote in Ted Kennedy's name as a substitute for George McGovern. I wanted Camelot again. I wanted a Kennedy in office, any Kennedy.

My political inclinations in those days were fostered by one chief concern, the concern for social justice. I had studied the Old Testament prophets and was persuaded that concern for the poor and the oppressed must be a passion for any serious Christian. I believed that the only viable instrument to bring about authentic social justice was the federal government. I was sadly aware that with great wealth comes great power and that the super-rich in this country were using their power to influence legislation that would favor their vested business interests. I was also convinced that the only way people ever got rich was by exploiting the poor. "One man's profit is another man's loss"—that was the myth that blinded me. In reality, although I knew something about theology, I was virtually ignorant of the most elementary principles of economics. My awakening came gradually. First I read William Simon's book, *A Time For Truth*. Simon's analysis of world economic problems and their root causes made me rethink the whole matter of the relationship between theology and economics. Further reading convinced me that some of my assumptions had been in serious error.

Two other major factors entered into my economic conversion. The first was my involvement in the Value of the Person Movement that focused on relationships between labor and management. My time spent in union halls and steel mills gave me a first-hand view of the struggle and pain of America's workers. I began to see that government policies were crippling both labor and management and bringing the nation's steel industry to its knees. Something was wrong. Radically wrong. I watched the poor get caught in the vise of soaring interest rates, mushrooming unemployment, and the sudden collapse of once vital industries. My philosophical bent drove me to seek causal answers.

The third factor in my conversion was the influence of my principal tutor in all things economic. My teacher was my son. From a young age he was fascinated and absorbed with economic theories. He devoured the complex writings of the Austrian-American genius Ludwig von Mises (1881–1973). My son kept asking me questions that I could not answer and supplying me with answers to questions I was not even asking. Finally I said to him, "You ought to write a book." So he did. What follows is what I believe to be a common-sense treatment of economic issues that directly affect each one of us. These issues involve our consciences as well as our wallets, our politics as well as our religious convictions. I hope that you will find the book instructive, challenging, and provocative.

R. C. Sproul
Ligonier, 1984

ACKNOWLEDGMENTS

Though still young, I have had the good fortune to have been influenced by many insightful people. My parents, who first suggested this project, showed great confidence in me, encouraged me, edited for me, supported my passion for books on the subject, and helped to provide a first rate education for me.

Mr. Henry Hildebrandt, teacher of history and economics at Wichita Collegiate School, sparked my interest with a strong dedication to both freedom and scholarship and provided a solid foundation.

My peers have also contributed heavily to this work. John Landsverk and Richard White share this interest with me and sharpened my thoughts through the clash of ideas. I would also like to thank Miss Heide Gyn for her support and inspiration.

ONE
HARD TIMES—
A CHRISTIAN APPROACH

A quick glance at any hometown newspaper shows our nation's concern with economics. Headlines follow unemployment levels, productivity figures, and inflation rates. Professional analysts interpret these figures to give us the economic forecast, sunny or cloudy, determined in great part by the analysts' political leanings. This onslaught of economic news, combined with television commentators, magazine reports, and today's bestselling economics books—Adam Smith's *Paper Money*, Milton Friedman's *Free to Choose*, and George Gilder's *Wealth and Poverty* leave many bewildered. What's the difference between the Laffer Curve and a sinking curve? Is the supply side your right side or your left side?

The confusion brought by this onslaught of economic data is mild compared to the personal distress experienced by the twenty-year veteran steelworker who loses his job. The unemployment rate hovers around the 8 percent mark nationwide and approaches 20 percent in certain highly industrialized pockets. This rate is not merely an abstract statistic suited for a ledger book or an obscure column in *The Wall Street Journal*. It is a rate that describes human pain. Unemployment hurts a person's pride as well as his pocketbook. It has become an alarming source of anguish to the American family. Of all economic statistics, this one hits home the most brutally.

The 1980 elections promised Americans a brave new future of

economic prosperity. Winning by a landslide margin, the incoming president promised a no-nonsense economic policy to rebuild the ailing, inflation-hounded economy. Reagan promised to balance the budget, to reduce taxes, to economize on the budget by cutting out the fat, and to reduce inflation. Inflation did go down, but taxes went up, the budget swelled, and the deficit hit record levels.* Unemployment increased with businesses cutting back or closing down altogether. Braniff Airlines, one of our nation's largest, was forced to declare bankruptcy. In the early eighties businesses were failing at a higher rate than during the early years of the Great Depression. Mercantilism, the age-old belief in economic nationalism, is threatening to put a halt to free international trade as laborers and executives alike beseech the government for economic protection from foreign competition. Japanese imports threaten many of America's once prosperous industries, with the automobile and steel industries suffering the heaviest competitive casualties.

Confusion mounts as Americans fear the worst, remembering the Great Depression and worrying about the future. The American dream seems as antiquated as a Horatio Alger novel. Our fear, however, seems empty and premature as we observe the economic circumstances abroad. The television beams pictures of starving children with grotesquely distorted stomachs and hollow eyes pleading for help. There are severe shortages of essential goods all over the world. Communist bloc citizens in the Soviet Union, Bulgaria, Hungary, and Czechoslovakia wait for hours in line to buy a meager portion of potatoes. Latin American peasants work without the advantages of adequate tools, adding sweat to their labor beyond the acceptable limits of Adam's curse. Inflation rates go over the 100 percent mark in Argentina, Israel, and Brazil. Exchange rates fluctuate dramatically. Nations plunge more deeply into debt. Economic confusion is not merely a Western phenomenon; it reaches all who wish to eat, to produce, to be good stewards of God's crea-

*The total amount of revenue taken in by the federal government has increased since the Carter administration. With inflation, wages go up, causing "bracket creep." Bracket creep occurs when wage earners find themselves in higher tax brackets with higher wages. Also, the 1982 Social Security reform caused higher taxation.

tion. Solutions to the confusion are varied and complex, a reality which only adds to the problem. The answers are not easy; neither are they impossible.

BIBLICAL ANSWERS

As popular interest in economic issue grows, Christians have been stimulated to seek biblical answers for economic ills that confront us in the atomic age. Christian bookstores display books expounding the Christian virtues of a socialist state or a theocratic free-market economy. There is a pitched battle in Christendom today fought by radical liberation theologians and militant theonomists (a group hoping for a return to much of Old Testament law), Democrats and Republicans, conservatives and liberals. All claim a concern for human well-being and for firmer biblical roots. Not all, however, are faithful to biblical and economic realities.

As Christians, we bear the responsibility of building a social order that reflects the glory of God. This responsibility reaches into the realm of sociology, political science, and economics. The Great Commission calls for the discipleship of all nations. We are called to bring the good news of the risen Christ to all and to bring all aspects of our lives under the rule of God. As Americans, we bear the responsibility of making our pledge of "one nation under God" a living reality, a social psalm of praise to God. Only a careful study of scriptural principles and a fervent effort to live by them can fulfill that pledge. This is no time for emotional slogan-writing and name-calling of our Christian brothers in different political-economic camps. We must study together, search out weaknesses and strengths in our own pet system, and strive to bear witness to the kingdom of God.

During any discussion of economics and politics from a biblical perspective, one will inevitably hear the oft-repeated phrase, "The Bible is not an economics textbook." No serious economist or theologian would deny this statement, but its implications are dangerous. The philosophical, moral, and ethical side of economics can easily be overlooked. That the Bible is not an economics textbook does not mean that it is totally useless for understanding economic issues. Economics—in theory, and especially in practice—touches heavily upon, and at times rudely collides with, biblical ethics. Where ethics touches economics, the Bible is relevant.

Biblical principles to guide economic study exist. Biblical law reaches the totality of life, so we should expect to find biblical principles of conduct for the individual, for the civil magistrate, and for a society. Scripture, though not a textbook, will not leave us groping in the dark, searching for ethical answers with nothing to guide our fallen minds. The Scripture is our guiding force, our given in the study of economics.

The Old Testament, for example, helps us understand the proper function of government and law, important issues in the study of economics. In the New Testament, Jesus dealt with the problem of the poor, the question of wealth, and the role of government. The apostles often dealt with similar questions. In the study of Christian economics, we do not turn first to Smith's *Wealth of Nations* nor to Marx's *Das Kapital*, but rather to the Word of God and the principles therein.

STEWARDSHIP

The first principle given to us from Scripture is *stewardship*. The concept of stewardship is at the root of the word *economics*. The Greek word *oikonomia*, "economics," literally means "house-law." Economics reaches beyond high-ranking economic advisors, bankers, and professors of economics to all of us who are stewards of this earth. More than the law of marginal utility, more than gross national products and national debts, economics is stewardship, an obligation given to all human beings at creation.

The Bible opens with the creation account. God did not simply rearrange or restructure pre-existent materials that were left hanging around from eternity. God was no celestial Columbus who discovered the universe and planted a divine flag on it. God brought forth our universe by the word of his mouth, out of nothing. He owns all things, not through rugged individualistic competition, but from the power of his word alone. His ownership cannot be contested with civil suits, tax men, or egalitarians seeking equal distribution between Yahweh, Allah, Baal, and Zeus. The universe is neither a corporation nor a partnership. It is a proprietorship, under the same ownership and management from the beginning of time. It is God who creates, and he owns the fruit of his labor.

On the sixth day God created man in his image. Man stood at the apex of the creation, Adam and Eve serving as God's vice-regents. God gave them dominion over the earth; they became his stewards. Their rights and privileges were attended by responsibilities and obligations.

Man was given work to do in this first dominion covenant. Adam's work was to dress, till, and keep the earth. This was an economic enterprise. It involved the tasks of production, labor, and stewardship. Note that this responsibility was given in the garden, before the fall. Labor was given as a gift, not as punishment; it must, therefore, be seen as part of the goodness of creation. Adam and Eve were invited to enjoy the garden, yet at the same time they were called to replenish and keep it.

After the fall and expulsion from the garden, Adam and Eve were still given rule over the earth despite their fallen nature. The earth continued to need rule and cultivation, and the mandate of dominion remained. Man's job is not finished yet. The call to subdue the earth and to be fruitful and multiply still stands despite stunning technological achievements and Malthusian cries of overpopulation. We must take this ancient injunction to heart if we are to be good stewards. We cannot hide our failure in subduing the earth (production) by putting a halt to our multiplying (reproduction). Man abides, and God's mandates abide with him.

God's call to stewardship requires hard work, efficient work, and a high regard for the earth God has given us. God's ownership demands that we care for the earth and use it to fulfill his purposes. We will be held accountable for how well we follow God's command of stewardship. We must acknowledge and act upon our role as vice-regents, as stewards bearing the image of God. We can have no ambivalence toward this role if we are to take charge as managers of God's creation in a positive and constructive manner. *Oikonomia* demands that we rule actively in God's house, carrying on the pledge of subduing the earth and being fruitful and multiplying.

PRIVATE OWNERSHIP

The principle of private ownership of property is woven throughout the Scriptures. True ownership of property includes control of that property. In modern fascist states individuals retain legal ownership on paper, but all control is dictated by the totalitarian regime. This is not only a modern phenomenon. Frédéric Bastiat, a French economist of the early nineteenth century, battled against government control of private property in his pamphlets *The Law* and *Economic Sophisms*. During Bastiat's time, the French weaving industry was shut down for an entire year as they waited for the bureaucratic word on how many threads per square inch they must use. The weavers held deeds to their factories; they simply didn't hold control.

Two events took place during the Exodus which illustrate the biblical notion of personal property. The first occurred at Mt. Sinai with the formulation of the Ten Commandments. The eighth commandment reads, "Thou shalt not steal." It seems to be a relatively simple commandment. It is deemed important enough by God to be elevated to the top ten precepts which establish the foundation of Israel's society.

It is not surprising that a foundational law code for a society would include prohibitions against killing and stealing. Respect for life and property have been built into countless civil law codes beyond the borders of Old Testament Israel. What is unusual, indeed extraordinary, about Israel's Decalogue is the content of the tenth commandment. How many architects of constitutional law would incorporate into their ten most axiomatic precepts a prohibition of inner lust for another person's property? Calvin sums up this prohibition by writing:

> Since the Lord would have the whole soul pervaded with love, any feeling of an adverse nature must be banished from our minds. The sum, therefore, will be, that no thought be permitted to insinuate itself into our minds, and inflame them with a noxious concupiscence tending to our neighbor's loss. . . . For if it was correctly said above, that under the words adultery and theft, lust and an intention to injure and

deceive are prohibited, it may seem superfluous afterwards to employ a separate commandment to prohibit a covetous desire of our neighbor's goods. [1]

Calvin rightly links the prohibition against coveting with the divine mandate to love our neighbor. Coveting and love are incompatible. Love demands that we refrain from stealing, injuring, despoiling, or even coveting our neighbor's private property. Still we ask, why is covetousness so heinous that it makes the top ten? Consider for a moment the fruits and consequences of human envy and covetousness. Lurking in the coveting heart is the impulse to theft, violence, vandalism, murder, and war. Eliminate these social ills from our culture, and we will have reduced human suffering enormously.

How can we make sense, for example, of vandalism? What does anyone gain by the act of wanton destruction of private or public property? The thief appropriates someone else's property for his own private use or sale, but in vandalism no one gains the property. It is either destroyed or defaced. Yet the vandal chooses to commit his act because it satisfies his hostility toward the property owner. Vandalism is covetousness gone wild. The creed of the vandal is simple, though devastating. He says, "If I cannot possess what you possess, I will destroy it so that you will not enjoy what I lack." The only gain is satisfied hatred.

Ownership of property is sanctioned by God, from the garden paradise to Abraham's flocks to the Promised Land to the tents of St. Paul.

LABOR AND PROPERTY

The Edenic lifestyle was not one of hanging around the garden, acquiring a tan, eating any legal fruit which might fall into one's hands, and chewing the fat with passing serpents. Adam and Eve were not models for travel brochures; they were called by God to work, to labor, to toil. This pre-fall calling gives dignity to labor. We were created for work. Luther demonstrated that all callings, within biblical legal bounds, were of value and a glory to God. Just as the church needs members with different gifts and skills, so also must our world have various forms of labor, interdependent and thus all valuable. A world full of ministers would have no churches, no bread for the Lord's Supper, and no printed Bible to read from. The kingdom of God is a kingdom of craftsmen.

Property is the normal result of labor. I find joy as I look out across the yard from the study window and see the fruit of two summers' labor. Green grass, budding trees, and young flowers make my expenditure of time and energy worthwhile. The fruit of my labor is my reward for carrying out the work mandate. God forbids theft and covetousness in order to protect this fruit.

But many Christian economic systems claiming biblical support do not give adequate place to God's mandate to stewardship. They view private ownership of property as an evil to combat, and they do not uphold the connection between work and reward. Such systems are well intentioned, but they can never solve today's economic woes. Today's worldwide problems require a strong solution, the very solution proposed by the One who created the world and who knows how it is supposed to operate.

TWO
SHOULD CHRISTIANS CARE
ABOUT THE MATERIAL WORLD?

For centuries the church has struggled with its understanding of the relationship between the physical and the spiritual, between the body and the soul. Two distortions have plagued us almost from the inception of the church. The twin enemies of biblical truth are radical materialism and radical spiritualism.

RADICAL MATERIALISM

Materialism is a view of life which regards the possession of material things as the highest good, the *summum bonum*. It involves more than a mere appreciation of physical things. It goes beyond the simple enjoyment of material benefits. It is both *radical* and an *ism*. It is radical because it makes material things the heart or "root" *(radix)* of all human happiness. It is an *ism* because it turns the neutral word *material* into a philosophy of life.

As an *ism*, materialism declares that the material is all there is. There is no spiritual dimension to life. The consistent materialist allows no room even for the existence of the spiritual. Thoughts and emotions are explained in terms of physical and chemical impulses. All of life is physical. If nothing apart from matter exists, it follows inexorably that nothing apart from the material has any value. Indeed even the word *value* must be given a physical meaning. Values are pure subjective emotional responses dictated by physical actions and reactions within the body, a Pavlovian slobbering induced by conditioned responses.

But, we say, there are no real materialists in the world, are there? Everyone surely recognizes that certain vital aspects of life are in fact spiritual and nonphysical. By no means. From before the time of Socrates right up to the twentieth century's B. F. Skinner, some serious philosophers have taken a radically materialistic view of life. It may be argued that none has been absolutely consistent. Even Skinner writes books, evidently trying to persuade his readers to change their thoughts through rational persuasion. (Unless of course he is counting on the chemical composition of the paper and ink of the printed page to do the job instead of the cogency of his argument.) His glaring inconsistency here is like that of the nihilist who declares that there are no values and then writes volumes to defend his own values and persuade others of them.

If radical materialists are few in number, and if even fewer achieve a consistency of their position, why should we worry about them? A cursory view of Western history should answer that question. The fallout from one philosopher's radical position can affect the lives of millions of people. Karl Marx's philosophical understanding of human history, *dialectical materialism*, directly affects two billion people and indirectly affects the whole world.

Not everyone thinks about materialism in the complex, philosophical manner in which Marx did. It is safe to assume that few people think in complex, philosophical ways at all. But people do think, and thinkers have viewpoints and value systems. Our value system may not be carefully thought out; we may not be able to articulate it. Yet we have values, and, more important, we live by them.

At the level of nonphilosophical living the world abounds with materialists. The radical sort influences the less radical and more benign sorts. But within the larger camp of materialists there are multitudes who believe that life consists of possessions and physical pleasures. Jesus' parable of the rich fool was not about a philosopher. It was about a farmer who lived as a materialist. His life was caught up in the pursuit of material goods to the point of woeful neglect of his soul. The man was probably not a *theoretical* materialist. He was a *practical* materialist. He lived as if he had no soul.

Practical materialism is seductive. It lures its victim with the hollow promise that the next acquisition, the next pay raise, the next windfall will deliver the prize of happiness. As it seduces, it preoccupies. In reflective moments the practical materialist acknowledges the reality of the spiritual realm and the importance of spiritual values. But he becomes so immersed in making a living that the spiritual is pushed aside by more pressing material concerns.

The stepchild of materialism is hedonism. This *ism* has appeared under various guises from the sophisticated to the crass. Its creed is simple. Good is equated with the pleasurable and evil with the painful. The goal of the hedonist is to maximize pleasure and minimize pain. The Epicureans who encountered St. Paul on Mars Hill in Athens were of this persuasion. Theirs was a cultured hedonism, a refined form of pleasure-seeking. Still, their creed was without hope: "Let us eat and drink, for tomorrow we die" (1 Cor. 15:32). The hedonist realized what the rich fool ignored, the imposing imminence of death. Yet his answer to life was no less foolish.

RADICAL SPIRITUALISM

The polar opposite of radical materialism is radical immaterialism or spiritualism. In this schema the root (radix) of reality is spiritual. From the incorporealists antedating Socrates to modern-day Christian Scientists, there have always been denials of, or severe depreciation of, physical reality. As with the materialists, many immaterialists have been more or less sophisticated. Some have adopted this perspective after careful philosophical analysis while others have accepted it uncritically.

At the practical level, the effect of spiritualism is to depreciate the physical as intrinsically imperfect at best or positively wicked at worst. Plato's valuing of the soul over the body, the idea over the imperfect physical copy, has had an enormous influence on Christian thought. Consider, for example, the chapter of monastic history where austere forms of rigorous self-denial, self-flagellation, and other forms of asceticism were elevated to the status of exalted virtues because of their antiphysical and therefore "spiritual" bent. The Roman Catholic dogma of the perpetual virginity of Mary was touched by this antiphysical perspective. Why else was Rome so zealous to perpetrate this doctrine apart form the assumption that even in the marriage state the sexual act was somehow tainted and would blemish the sacred character of the virgin?

Even modern moral theologians argue at times that sex within marriage is at best a necessary evil whose only moral justification is to reproduce the species. Sex is evil primarily because it is physical. But sexual taboos are only a small part of the influence of spiritualism. It breeds a "taste not, touch not" mentality that reduces the kingdom of God to matters of eating and drinking, focusing on physical externals as the mark of "true spirituality," a paradoxical measuring rod indeed. Even in our Playboy-saturated culture the cult of the perpetual virgin lives on. Poverty is glorified and physical pleasure and beauty are vilified. To love art, music, food, clothes, or private property is to be "worldly." The Roman Bacchanalia is traded in for the hermitage.

A BIBLICAL ALTERNATIVE

Materialism and spiritualism breed on each other's extremes, fostering endless actions and reactions to each other. The great myth they represent is that we must choose between them. They scream at us, "Either/or, either/or." But we are not left to choose between two distortions. Scripture offers another option.

The Bible views the material world as the good creation of God. More is involved with this judgment than the simple declaration that "God saw that it was good" (Gen. 1). Unlike the Greek, the Old Testament Jew viewed creation as a *voluntary* action of God. According to the Bible the world did not evolve or emanate from some eternal substance. Rather God chose to create it by divine fiat. The implications of that for the value of material things are staggering. God chose to create a material world. He decided, within the framework of his own divine mind, to make a world with food and drink and sex in it. Indeed he circumscribed the use of these physical things by his righteous law. They were created good. They were included in man's fall. They are integral parts of man's redemption.

The Greek's future hope was redemption *from* the body. The Christian's future hope is redemption *of* the body. The Greek viewed the body as the prison-house of the soul. The Christian views the body as the temple of the Holy Spirit. The Greek viewed material things as being intrinsically imperfect. The Christian views them as good things created by God, though capable of sinful use and abuse.

One teaching of Jesus has been oft distorted to support a false dichotomy between body and soul. We read his solemn words in Matthew 10:28: "Fear not them which kill the body, but are not able to kill the soul: but rather fear him which is able to destroy both soul and body in hell." Some have erroneously concluded that Jesus is here making a value judgment of the relative worth of the body to the soul. They infer, "Don't worry about the body. What counts is the soul."

Jesus makes no such inference. The contrast he establishes has nothing to do with the value of the body over against that of the soul. The contrast is between two powers that evoke fear in us, the power of men and the power of God. The one who can kill the body but not the soul is man. The one who has the power to kill both body and soul is God. Man's power to harm us is limited to killing the body. The same limit does not apply to God. It is also significant here that Jesus' view of the soul differs from the traditional Greek view of the indestructibility of the soul. In Jesus' view the soul is mortal. It is capable of death. It has what Augustine called the *posse mori.* It cannot be destroyed by man, but it can be destroyed by God. This does not mean that God will destroy the soul as the annihilationists maintain, but merely that he can.

Redemption, in the full biblical sense of the word, is both physical and spiritual. The Bible knows of no divorce between ministering to the physical and spiritual needs of people. The two may be distinguished but never separated. There is, to be sure, a difference between evangelism and material welfare programs, but they are to go together.

Recent Christian history has witnessed an unnatural split between these two dimensions of Christian concern. Nineteenth-century liberalism (a distinctive theological movement in the history of Christianity) provoked a crisis by opting for materialism. If, as the liberals supposed, there was no historical resurrection, no virgin birth, no atoning death, no ascension, no miracles, then what is the abiding significance of Christianity in a modern world? What is the church's mission?

The liberal church faced difficult options. It could forthrightly apologize to the world for more than eighteen hundred years of propagating error and say, "We're sorry, world, we were wrong. Jesus is dead and we have misled you with our preaching, our teaching, our music, and our art." This option may be preferred by those with a consistent posture of integrity. Some liberal scholars, to their credit, in fact adopted it and left the ministry. It is, however, a radical option and one not very practical for large numbers of clergy to choose. It means closing the churches, absorbing a monumental financial loss, abandoning a powerful institution of social change, and going out of business.

The liberal church's second option was to focus attention on the "relevant" abiding virtue of Christianity, its ethical system. The church, after all, was indeed a powerful human institution that was in a position to influence millions of people in the area of social concern. Salvation could not be focused on this world without throwing in matters of life after death, personal justification, and reconciliation with an angry God by means of some cosmically loaded vicarious sacrifice on a cross. Of course, this all required not only a shift in focus or emphasis of the message of Jesus, but also a massive revision of the content of the New Testament. Scholars sought to penetrate the true essence of Christianity, stripped of its mythical or punitive baggage. What emerged was a "social gospel" that reduced Christianity to concern for man's present suffering in this space-time world. Now the agenda was to carry out Jesus' mandate of feeding the hungry, giving shelter to the homeless and clothes to the naked, and caring for the prisoner, the widow, the orphan, and all who are poor and oppressed. Christianity was now seen as an ethical force with a social-action agenda. The traditional gospel with its emphasis on supernatural, miraculous redemption centering on the person and work of Christ was not negotiable.

This second option left some sticky ethical problems for liberal churchmen. Most central was the thorny question of honesty in professions of ordination vows and subscription to traditional creeds and confessions. But these problems could be artfully dodged by redefining religious language and by gradually changing the content and status of creedal formulations. The confessions were soon relegated to the status of interesting, but not binding, museum pieces.

Not everyone in the church shared the skepticism toward the supernatural that was part and parcel of the liberal movement. Conservatives fought fiercely to retain the classical Christology and biblical gospel. Certain "fundamentals" of faith were considered utterly non-negotiable. The story controversy that followed at the beginning of the twentieth century left mainline Protestant denominations sorely divided. For the most part the liberals won the day, capturing the strategic seminaries, colleges, and hierarchical positions in the churches and leaving a protracted series of often bitter splinter groups seeking to establish new churches committed to the traditional emphasis of the gospel.

During this stormy controversy, the label *evangelical* underwent a significant historical change in nuance. Originally the term was used as a virtual synonym for *Protestant*, taking its cue from the Reformation principle of "justification by faith alone." After the modernist-fundamentalist controversy the term began to signify that group which believed in personal eternal salvation and which practiced forms of evangelism that called people to personal faith in a divine Christ who made a substitutionary-sacrificial atonement and was raised bodily from the grave. (The ideas of deity, atonement, and resurrection were also integral aspects of Roman Catholic theology that, in their essence, were not in dispute during the Reformation).

The evangelical had a new identity and, consequently, a new agenda. He was fighting so hard to retain the gospel of personal salvation as well as his supernatural understanding of Christ that he doubled his emphasis on evangelism, at times to the exclusion of social concern. Here is where the unnatural division occurred. Many thought that the social-action agenda of liberalism and the biblical literalism of conservatism were essentially incompatible. Evangelicals tended to avoid social reform, now considered a "liberal" concern, for fear of being tarred with a liberal brush. Thus in rejecting liberalism many evangelicals uncritically rejected social concern, ignoring the biblical mandate for it and the rich evangelical heritage of involvement in it.

The pendulum has swung back. A new social consciousness has arisen among evangelicals that has sparked new interest in social action. The debate now among evangelicals is not so much whether social action is an integral dimension of biblical Christianity but what kind of social action is biblically mandated.

We must also point out in passing through this brief historical reconnaissance that another label used by evangelicals has also undergone a significant linguistic metamorphosis. The term *fundamentalist* has changed dramatically in the last seventy-five years. The term was coined by serious conservative scholars who entered the debate with liberal scholars concerning the essence of Christianity. The fundamentals were the classic doctrines that conservatives believed were the *sine qua non* of historic Christianity. They included doctrines confessed by virtually every church in the World Council of Churches. In 1900 an orthodox Roman Catholic would have agreed with conservative Protestants on most of the fundamentals.

Over the ensuing decades, however, the term *fundamentalist* took on nuances of anti-intellectualism, legalism, Arminianism, and pietism. Today many followers of orthodox Christianity disavow the term *fundamentalist* even though they ardently adhere to the classic fundamentals. Fundamentalism as a subculture of evangelicalism exhibits a tendency toward world-denial that may obscure the biblical attitude toward physical things. The spirit of Manichaeism lives on, equating the biblical judgment on sinful "flesh" as an implied denigration of all things physical. But even a cursory reading of Scripture affirms that we live in a physical world created by God and that God is profoundly concerned with our bodily lives.

From Genesis to Revelation the God of Scripture holds out promises of material welfare. Abraham, by divine covenant pledge, was promised that his nation would receive land and property. He became one of the wealthiest men of antiquity, rivaled only by the patriarch Job. The Exodus had profound economic overtones. God delivered a people oppressed as a slave-labor force, a people forced into destitute poverty. They were delivered to a land God promised would be flowing with milk and honey, a land where the people could prosper and enjoy the benefits of physical well-being.

The imagery of heaven found in Revelation is replete with signs of physical prosperity and opulence. The new heaven and the new earth, indicating a renovated created order, are crystallized in the description of the new Jerusalem. This city, which comes down from heaven, is adorned with the radiance of rare jewels. It is a city of pure gold with walls of jasper. The foundations are bedecked with precious stones including sapphires, emeralds, topaz, and amethysts. The gates are made of pearls and the street of gold. The provision of food is a gourmet's delight.

It can certainly be argued that the apocalyptic description above is symbolic and not intended to be taken literally. But the fact remains that the Bible uses images of extreme opulence to describe heaven. If these riches were under God's judgment, they would hardly be used as symbols of ultimate glory.

The tabernacle and temple structures of the Old Testament were certainly not mere symbols. By divine instruction that included fine details, an exquisite structure was made for the sanctuary. A taste of the details may be found in Exodus 25:1–8.

> And the LORD spake unto Moses, saying, Speak unto the children of Israel, that they bring me an offering: of every man that giveth it willingly with his heart ye shall take my offering. And this is the offering which ye shall take of them; gold, and silver, and brass, and blue, and purple, and scarlet, and fine linen, and goats' hair, and rams' skins dyed red, and badgers' skins, and shittim wood, oil for the light, spices for anointing oil, and for sweet incense, onyx stones, and stones to be set in the ephod, and in the breastplate. And let them make me a sanctuary; that I may dwell among them.

These items for the wilderness tabernacle pale in comparison with the splendors of the temple built in Jerusalem. The temple was an authentic wonder of the ancient world, its glory dwarfing even that of the cathedral of Notre Dame de Paris or St. Peter's Basilica in Rome.

All these luxurious items were capable of abuse. Indeed, the judgment of God fell on the temple. Israel's silver became dross and its gold tarnished. But there remains a place for these things in God's kingdom. In themselves they are not to be despised. The biblical view assigns value to the body and the soul, to evangelism and social concern, to the spiritual and the material. Redemption is for the whole man.

THREE
WHERE PROSPERITY COMES FROM

Economics, to the uninitiated, can sometimes appear incomprehensible. Many, after seeing top experts disagree, assume that they cannot possibly understand it. Yet although economics is complex at times, its basic principles are universally intelligible. It is imperative that we have a rudimentary understanding of the science, for it is the study of why there is daily bread on our tables.

Economists study a maze of interconnected forces, trying to discover the root principles operating in them. Is there an order in the marketplace where supply meets demand and commerce takes place? Adam Smith, history's first economist, devised the "invisible hand theory." Simply put, the invisible hand is the force that takes the combined interests of all members of society and creates a well-ordered marketplace.

For Smith, economic forces follow a kind of natural law, a dynamic of checks and balances that function without the necessity of government interference or manipulation. Basic laws such as the law of supply and demand work to keep the marketplace growing. The principles of self-interest balanced by free competition work best to promote society's interest. Smith understood the reality of sinful human greed but argued that the individual, while promoting his own interest in a free and competitive marketplace, frequently promoted the interest of society "more effectually than when he really intends to promote it."[2] For example, Henry Ford undoubtedly wished to accumulate wealth. At the same time, many people wanted cheap and accessible transportation. Through this combination, the Model T was born.

Smith's thought lies behind much conservative economic thought. He is opposed by those who, following the thought of John Maynard Keynes, put the accent on government regulation of economics. Their theory is that government manipulation, whether by stimulation or restraint, can produce a more ordered and prosperous society than that achieved by the blind forces of nature working in an essentially free market.

Conservatives see the shift from a commerce-oriented marketplace to a politicized marketplace as a disaster for economic growth and prosperity. They argue that what results is a stranglehold on entrepreneurial growth and expansion. If Henry Ford were alive today, they say, he would never get past government bureaucratic paperwork. Maybe Detroit would have been zoned "residential," or perhaps Mr. Ford would have spent his life doing an environmental impact study for the EPA. Perhaps the Model T would have been found "unsafe at any speed." Whatever the case, if Henry Ford had worked under today's restrictions, everyone could have expected a few more years of transportation in the surrey with the fringe on top. According to economic conservatives, the invisible hand leaves a well-ordered market with satisfied producers and satisfied consumers, whereas the highly visible hand of government manipulation leaves welts and bruises on the market and thus on the producer and consumer.

In cutting through the complexities of economics we search for the most basic and elementary principles that cause economic expansion and contraction. We know that the intricacies of action and reaction are vast and difficult to sort out. If ever there was a science where the forest could be lost in the trees, it is the science of economics. For example, if a farmer's corn crop in Iowa is destroyed by a hailstorm, the repercussions are literally worldwide. The smaller corn crop would drive prices up. Corn used as feed then drives up livestock prices. Higher livestock prices could cause many in China to eat less meat and more rice, thus causing a rice shortage in China.

We are searching for root causes, for "forest-size" causes that affect our economic world. We are trying to go back to ground zero to seek what philosophers call the *necessary conditions* for something to take place.

A necessary condition is that without which something cannot occur. For example, oxygen is a necessary condition for fire, since without oxygen there can be no fire. However, oxygen is not a sufficient condition for fire. Oxygen *alone* cannot bring forth a fire. A sufficient condition is a condition that is powerful enough, by itself, to cause a given effect.

There are certain necessary conditions for material prosperity. Only their active use and proper combination can bring forth the desired end, material prosperity. Our quest is for the bedrock factors, the non-negotiables of economic growth. What conditions must exist for economic growth and material welfare to happen?

The first necessary condition for material welfare is *production*. Without production there are no man-made material goods for our benefit. Man can seek to exist by depending on nature's production: he can dwell in caves, forage for wild fruits and berries, and kill wildlife for food and clothing. But even these primitive forms of survival methods demand some sort of human production. Primitive tools used for hunting, fishing, cooking, and building are themselves *products*. They may be crudely fashioned from stone or wood, but they are nevertheless products.

Modern material needs involve lumber and bricks for houses, agricultural goods for food, and fabric for clothing. Food, shelter, clothing, medicine: these compose the essential products for survival. They all require production. Without production we perish. Production is a necessary condition, a non-negotiable, a *sine qua non* of our material welfare.

It is possible to have production without material welfare if the efforts of production are geared toward useless products. The production of square-wheeled cars, for example, adds little if anything to a nation's wealth. For a nation to prosper, production must be of usable goods.

The second necessary condition for material welfare is the development of *tools*. Because tools enable a person to produce more products at faster rates, they are necessary for increased productivity. Our American steel producers lag behind their Japanese competitors precisely because the Japanese have newer and better tools which enable them to produce superior steel at a lower cost. Leonard Reed, president of the Foundation of Economic Education, uses a pencil to illustrate the necessity of tools. Reed points out that no individual person left alone on an island could produce a single pencil like the one I am using now, even if he spent a lifetime trying. Yet the hourly production rate of pencils in America is staggering, due primarily to the sophisticated use of tools.

The third necessary condition for material welfare is *surplus capital*. To buy tools I must have surplus or investment capital. Without the capital I cannot buy the tools; and without the tools, I cannot increase my production. Without production I cannot achieve material welfare. Yet surplus capital alone is not a sufficient condition for wealth. Surplus capital could be used to invest in tools to produce square-wheeled cars, which do nothing for man's material welfare. Surplus capital must be invested in tools which are used for increased production of goods in demand.

The fourth necessary condition for material welfare is *profit*. Surplus capital cannot exist without profit. Profit, though much maligned, is a key to material prosperity because it creates surplus capital. Profit exists when income is greater than expenditure. This simple relationship is at the root of prosperity: profit becomes surplus capital, which allows investment in tools for increased production, which in turn produces material prosperity. Of course, profit alone cannot increase prosperity. It can sit idly or be spent wastefully. Wasteful consumption may be due to foolishness, greed, or attempts to avoid excessive taxation. Inflation may induce people to consume rather than to save. Profit invested in unwanted goods does not help man's material welfare. Yet prudent investment of profit is the force behind increased wealth.

This discussion of the necessary conditions for wealth may be better explained with an illustration.

Taking away one of these necessary conditions and expecting economic success is like expecting a one-legged man to walk. It simply cannot be done. To enjoy material blessings, and to help

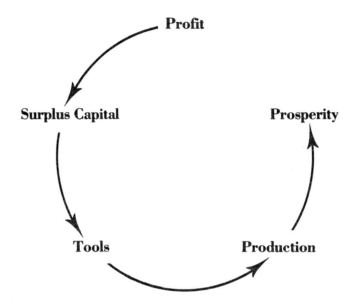

the poor, Christians must protect these forces from hindrance. To protect them we must first understand them and study them.

Let us use Leonard Reed's pencil example to see how production relates to material welfare. We can begin by imagining that on our Robinson Crusoe's eightieth birthday he completes a pencil. If he is working at $3.35 an hour, labor costs for one pencil reach more than $400,000.00 (assuming sixty years of work at forty hours a week.) Today one can buy a pencil for ten cents. All this is due to mass production.

In any given production endeavor there are fixed costs. These costs include the cost of land and tools. Whether one produces one pencil or one thousand, these costs remain the same. Relative costs are those which change with each additional unit of output. These include raw materials and natural resources. The relative cost of each additional unit is usually low. This low relative cost means that mass produced items tend to be inexpensive. As a result, we have an abundance of cheap pencils in America today while Robinson Crusoe has only one. Mass production has allowed this book to be written and a copy to reach your hands.

Mass production in the factory brought on the Industrial Revolution. Though we tend to associate the Industrial Revolution with poor housing and deplorable working conditions for the working classes, we should remember that in spite of these conditions, the proletariat came in droves from the farmlands to work in the factories. Factories engaged in mass production to supply the demands of the workers. Mass production allowed the common man to have luxuries once owned only by nobles.

It is the poor that reap the benefits of mass production. Mass production strengthens the economy and provides more jobs. Increased production also benefits the poor by making necessities more accessible. Consider the case of a peasant cotton farmer in an underdeveloped nation. Suppose he is thirty years old, six feet tall, one hundred and eighty pounds, and of superior intelligence. Imagine at the same time a Mississippi Delta farmer of the same age but smaller, physically weaker, and less intelligent than the third-world peasant. Why is it that the Delta farmer produces a hundred times more cotton than the peasant? The answer is not found in brute strength, personal industry, or intelligence quotients. The answer lies with the tools. Tools make mass production possible. While the peasant works with his hands, the Delta farmer uses an air-conditioned, stereo-equipped John Deere tractor and cotton gin. His land is fertilized with highly developed nutrients. His cotton is processed in mechanized plants and shipped to the marketplace. The peasant must invest weeks of labor to produce enough cotton for a single shirt; the Delta farmer supplies enough cotton for many shirts every day.

The value to the poor of mass production—production by sophisticated tools supplied by surplus capital—is the *lower cost per unit of the produced goods*. A single shirt is now affordable by most people in developed nations, although this is not true where mass production is not used. So it goes with food, shelter, and even medicine. (I once spoke to a medical missionary who ministered to a primitive tribe in the interior of Africa whose lives were ravaged by disease, infant mortality, and malnutrition. He said, "The lives of these people are significantly enhanced by a bottle of aspirin tablets!")

Today in America we are in the throes of a productivity crisis. This crisis hurts all of us as prices increase along with the length of unemployment lines. When production falls, so does our material welfare. Between the years 1948 and 1954, output (production) per man-hour increased by 4 percent annually. Between 1956 and 1974 the annual increase had plummeted to 2.1 percent. In the years 1970 through 1974 the increase stood at only 1.6 percent annually. By 1980, for the first time in American history, our productivity actually decreased. According to William Simon, writing in *A Time For Truth*, since 1960 the United States has ranked last in productivity growth among eight major industrialized nations. The once robust United States economy has grown weak on a diet of excessive taxation, monetary inflation, and governmental regulations. No economy can survive long, let alone grow, in such an environment.

Productivity is more than an abstract word used by demanding executives and scientists. Productivity goes beyond pragmatic growth programs. It goes beyond being a key to material welfare. We are called to be productive by God. Productivity is a spiritual and ethical obligation. God commands that we "bear fruit," that our work be worthwhile. Paul's exhortation that those who do not work shall not eat (2 Thess. 3:10) illustrates our obligation to produce. We are to bear fruit so that our hungry can be fed, so that our nation may be blessed with prosperity.

For any production to take place, three things are necessary: time, energy, and money. I reached an understanding of this as a teenager at the family dinner table. Our grass had been quite productive during springtime and as a result needed to be cut. My father explained that he had neither the time nor the energy to perform the task. He was, however, prepared to reward me handsomely with his money in exchange for my youthful abundance of energy and time. It was the start of a prosperous business relationship. The landscape was enhanced as well. My father supplied the lawnmower. The lack of a mower would have altered the relationship dramatically. The time and energy used in cutting the grass would have increased a hundredfold if I had had to cut the grass with a pair of scissors or, worse yet, with my front teeth. To make it worth my while, my wage would have had to increase significantly.

The lawnmower is a relatively simple and inexpensive tool, yet it enables work to be done more easily, more quickly, and at a lower cost. One simple tool gave my family a beautiful yard, me a relatively painless job, and my father an inexpensive laborer. It saved me time and energy while it saved my father money. That small amount of money saved could improve the all-around economy in various ways. It could be spent elsewhere to help someone else's business or it could be invested, privately or through a bank, to finance more tools elsewhere in the economy.

We have seen that tools are necessary, but who should own them? Should private individuals own tools, or should tools belong to a collective government? In any given production endeavor, it is tools which carry the most weight. The common equation "land plus labor *times* tools" emphasizes the importance of tools to production. Control of tools is the key to production. As a rambunctious young boy I often participated in neighborhood games of baseball. Because they were unorganized games with no official umpire, there were many disputed calls. If the debate over a call could not be resolved, the matter was turned over for final decision to the tool owner, the child who provided the bat and the ball. This boy was the highest authority, because he had the power to halt play completely by going home, bat and ball in hand. Here I learned the axiom, "He who controls the tools controls the game."

Karl Marx had much to say about the ownership of the means of production. The Communist movement is rooted in two basic assumptions concerning tools. Marx's theory of surplus value stated that profit is the theft of the worker's fruit of his labor. He argued that all the value in a given product lies in that which the worker puts into it. In effect, the laborer receives wages equal to the value he produces in only a fraction of his working day. The remaining value, produced in the rest of his working day, is skimmed off the top, stolen by the propertied class. This goes beyond poor working conditions and low wages in and of themselves. It is exploitation of the worker.

To redress such exploitation, Marx called for national ownership of the means of production. He regarded private ownership as an evil causing the misery of the working class. Marx failed to see the true source of economic value. Value is determined, not by man-hours, but by the desires of the consumer. The sun-roof umbrella illustrates this principle. The process of producing such an item would no doubt necessitate long and strenuous labor. However, consumers would be expected to pay little for it despite the enormous "value" instilled in it by the producers' blood, sweat, and tears.

The producer bets that his product will be in great demand. He invests his money in the tools of production, hoping he can satisfy the needs or whims of the buying public. Profit results when the consumer places a value on a given item higher than the cost of producing the item. Tools keep the cost low and the profit high. Marx failed to see the actual role of tools in the production process. Tools save both the bourgeoisie and the proletariat time, energy, and money.

Government ownership of the means of production has not alleviated the misery of the common worker. If anything, it tends to increase it. Government cannot be efficient and work properly in the marketplace, because it is an agent of force. And because it cannot use the pricing mechanism as a gauge of supply and demand, it need not make a profit, it need not be efficient, it need not be productive. The struggling Conrail railroad system illustrates the point.

We live in an era of rapid technological growth. Modern science is meeting the demands for newer and better tools. The computer, the word processor, and better forms of communication are increasing efficiency in the office. In the factory, robotics is growing, causing some to cheer and many to worry that this new form of automation will raise unemployment. Such fear is not new. Throughout history many have decried machines for taking away jobs. Yet the record indicates the opposite: increased productivity increases employment. To be sure, specific jobs are lost, and some people are forced to relocate their employment. That is often a severe though temporary cost of increased production. But if we followed the idea that machines cause unemployment to its logical conclusion, our goal would be to return to our primitive state, eking out a living without so much as a flint and stone to give us warmth. Surely we would have full-scale employment, but at the same time we would have full-scale starvation.

Shipping was once the leading industry of the northeastern United States. The industry centered on whaling, since oil processed from whales was the leading commercial substance used in lamps to illumine American homes. Then almost overnight the industry went belly-up. What happened? A Mr. Drake dug a hole in Titusville, Pennsylvania, and discovered oil. The first commercial use of the new "black gold" was kerosene, a cheap and efficient fuel for oil lamps. While oil men experienced a boom and produced a generation of Jed Clampetts, things were bad in New England. Harpooners were suddenly out of work, their skill no longer an economic necessity. But the kerosene boom itself was short-lived. The oil industry was suddenly threatened by a man named Tom Edison who said, "A pox on all your oil lamps." Unemployment hit the kerosene plants, but business was soon booming at Sylvania and General Electric.

Fortunately for the oil tycoons, they received a stay of economic execution. The combustion engine and Henry Ford used new forms of production that insured a lucrative future for oilmen. But still the harpooners were out of work, and so, very rapidly, were blacksmiths. One wonders what would have happened had the government poured money into salvaging the whaling industry or restrained the building of cars or light bulbs.

Temporary or short-range unemployment can be caused by ill-begotten production endeavors as people produce that which is not in demand. This is quickly eliminated as workers find jobs in areas of production where there is demand. Wagon makers were hurt by Henry Ford's introduction of the cheap automobile. These workers, however, were quickly reabsorbed into the nation's workforce in automobile production and other new industries. Certainly today's auto industry with its vast array of related production endeavors employs far more people than did its predecessor, the horse-and-buggy industry. We can plainly see that man always has unlimited desires. We cannot produce and produce until we want no more. We will continue fulfilling our desires as long as we can afford to do so. But when governmental interference keeps the cost artificially high, we have unemployment. The minimum wage puts an artificially high price on meeting some demands. If a particular form of labor is not worth $3.35 to an employer, no one is hired.

Let us imagine that I own a factory which produces corrugated paper boxes. I am a person who enjoys cleanliness, but I am not a fanatic about it. I think that it would be helpful to hire someone to clean the floors of my factory. I would be willing to pay someone $2.50 to do this simple chore. The government, however, forces me to pay nearly $5.00 (minimum wage, unemployment insurance, social security, etc.). It is not worth $5.00 an hour to me to have my floor clean; hence no one is hired, and someone—the low-skill person whom the minimum wage was designed to protect—is out of work.

I know of no present automaton which is able to sweep floors by itself. Automation does not take jobs from the market, but rather allows mass production which in turn raises employment. Let us illustrate with a historical example. Sir Richard Arkwright invented his cotton spinning machine in 1760. At that time in England there were approximately 5,200 spinners and 2,700 weavers using spinning wheels. In all, 7,900 labored in the production of cotton textiles. Arkwright's invention met bitter opposition as workers feared their jobs. The opposition was so violent it had to be put down by force. In 1787, only twenty years after Arkwright's invention, Parliament studied the number of those actively spinning and weaving cotton. The study revealed 320,000 persons earning their living spinning and weaving as compared to 7,900 only twenty years earlier. That represents an increase of 4,400 percent.

Even today many economists support the fallacy that automation hurts employment rates. Some economists are concerned about the booming computer industry. They claim that it will cause a loss of jobs in our country, that it decreases the demand for labor. The economist apparently concludes that we can maximize jobs by making labor inefficient and unproductive.

An economics teacher once shared with his class his plan for full employment. He told us that the way to end unemployment is extremely simple: we must simply eliminate the wheel. Every unemployed or underemployed man, woman, and child could then be hired to carry wheat on his or her back from the heartland to all around the country. No more trucks, cars, trains, bikes, or airplanes without the wheel. Without the wheel we would enjoy full employment, but we would struggle to attain the bare necessities of life.

Tools are the force behind production. They save the producer time, energy, and money. These savings allow mass production at low cost, which in turn allows the common man to experience treasures never dreamed of before the Industrial Revolution. The ownership and control of tools constitutes control of the production process. Private control tends toward efficiency, while bureaucratic government control brings inefficiency and a distortion of the market process. The Communist experiment in Russia shows us misery and starvation, not a worker's paradise. A study of history shows the vast difference in material welfare between economies based on private industry and those based on government control. Automation leads to higher, more efficient production. While it may temporarily dislocate jobs, in the end it leads to higher employment. Tools work, and they must be protected from interference if we are to enhance our material welfare.

My grandfather often delights in explaining to me the way things were before I was born. Before the advent of power steering, truck drivers generally had arms large enough to make Charles Atlas envious. Turning the wheels of such large trucks was no easy task. Today, Charles Atlas's mythical ninety-seven-pound weakling could turn the wheel of the largest trucks with relative ease. Truck driving is open to more men and also to women because of a tool— the powered steering wheel. The most monstrous man in a pre-power-steering truck was far less efficient than a ninety-seven-pound weakling in a more modern truck. Physical strength is no match for superior tools.

Archimedes, the ancient Greek mathematician and physicist, understood this point long before Adam Smith walked the earth. Archimedes did not say, "Give me arms strong enough and I shall move the world," but rather "Give me a lever big enough, and I shall move the world." Tools can have the strength of a thousand

men, and they never get tired. Some may bemoan the loss of seeing
the big truck driver flexing his big arms as he makes a turn. I cheer
the new freedom of power steering and leave the big arms for Charles
Atlas.

The desire to work hard alone cannot bring us higher productivity. Just as physical strength is no match for good tools, an industrious spirit alone cannot beat good tools for higher production.
Even if we give great industrial zeal to our strong man driving the
ancient truck, the weak man in the modern truck would remain
more efficient and productive. Although zeal and physical strength
are desirable, tools are the most potent and necessary ingredient in
productivity.

Tools do not grow on trees. Modern tools are often intricate,
delicate, and expensive. One cannot walk into the local hardware
store and ask for a bottle-capping machine. Tools must be made to
order, to do their assigned jobs in a particular place in a production
line in a given factory. Tools must be tailored to their individual
purpose. Industrial tools, for the most part, cannot be mass-produced, and therefore their costs run quite high. At the same time,
the demand for tools is enormous. To stay in business, an owner
must keep abreast of the latest technology, to continue to grow in
efficiency. As a result of this great demand, and the high value
placed on large industrial tools, they tend to be very expensive. It
is here that we see the initial role of surplus capital. Surplus capital
is money put aside for the purpose of investment in tools. Surplus
capital is essential for a company to compete and to grow. Any
attack on surplus capital is of necessity finally an attack on productivity and, therefore, on the material prosperity of the nation as a
whole. Erosion of surplus capital does damage that no social program can fix. Those concerned with material welfare cannot overlook this and must work to protect surplus capital.

The Japanese today incur the wrath of many Americans. Recently a Japanese autoworker in America was killed by an American member of the United Auto Workers. There are reports of
foreign cars being destroyed by "patriotic" Americans. The simple
fact is that the Japanese are outcompeting us. The Japanese produce better cars, better steel, better motorcycles, and better radios.

Are they to be blamed? Is an American to be blamed for purchasing a superior product? Japanese quality is often attributed to their industrious spirit, their lower wages, and their lifetime hiring practices. The most crucial factor, however, is that the Japanese have superior tools. Their auto industry has far more robotic equipment and other tools than our own. These superior tools are made possible through one thing—investment capital. From the sixties through the early seventies, private investment in the United States averaged less than 18 percent of the gross national product per year. During that same period, Japan averaged almost twice that amount with 35 percent per year. That kind of investment and a desire to serve the consumer makes a company profitable. From the sixties to the early seventies, the United States was lowest in capital investment among all industrialized nations. We must remember that since 1960 the United States has ranked last in productivity growth among the eight major industrialized nations also. The correlation is obvious.

These are not irrelevant statistics. This is bread and butter. We, as a nation, are not fulfilling the biblical mandate to bear fruit. It is not simply a case of a nation resting on its economic laurels, but rather of a nation suffering from governmental policies that discourage the accumulation of surplus capital. Without the surplus capital there can be no tools. Without newer and better tools, our productivity, our fruit-bearing, is dealt a fatal blow.

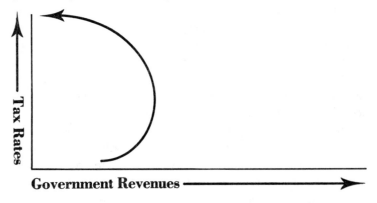

THE LAFFER CURVE

While one can plainly see that taxation hurts the accumulation of surplus capital, it is also quite apparent that many producers pay little or no taxes at all through the use of tax shelters. It appears that investment is not taking place because so much money is poured into frivolous tax shelters. It appears that wasteful consumption is the culprit responsible for our declining productivity. The effect of taxation and money put into shelters is essentially the same: money taxed or sheltered cannot be used for productive purposes. Economist Arthur Laffer, supporter of the new supply side economics, introduced a solution to the problem. The Laffer Curve illustrates the effects of taxation. Laffer suggests that two different tax rates produce the same amount of income. A 0 percent tax rate brings no income. A 100 percent tax rate brings no income either, as all taxable activity ceases due to a lack of motivation. In like manner, a 10 percent tax rate brings in the same amount of money as a 90 percent rate. The lower tax rate could bring in sufficient income to run the government and still give people the incentive to save and be productive. Conspicuous consumption, the spending of great wealth on frivolities and baubles, would cease and more money would be poured into the production process. Paralyzing money that could be used in production is deadly whether it be through taxation or tax shelters. Wasteful consumption does not come through stupidity or greed, but rather from governmental practices of taxation and inflation that make it unprofitable to save money—money needed for tools, tools needed for productivity, productivity which brings material prosperity. The Laffer Curve cuts the Gordian knot of government growth and private stagnation. However, both taxation and tax shelters are increasing in America today.

Tools are the key ingredient in production, more important than physical strength and an industrious spirit. Tools cost money, often a great deal of money, due to the great demand for them and the fact that they usually cannot be mass-produced. We have seen how effectively tools work in the strong and growing economy of Japan. We have looked at the relationship of a high rate of saving to acquiring tools. We have also examined some obstacles to the accumulation of surplus capital, particularly the government policies that make spending money more profitable than saving it. These policies hurt savings, which hurts the development of tools, which in turn hurts our production capabilities.

Profit is essential to material prosperity. It is at the base of those factors which are non-negotiables for material prosperity. It is an absolutely necessary condition for material welfare, inasmuch as it allows savings for investment in tools which allow production which gives us wealth. Without profit, there is no money for investment.

Profit is more than one company's balance. It is also a family's balance. If a family spends less than it earns, that is profit. This profit can be turned back into the family. The breadwinner or winners could invest the money in their education, making their skills more marketable. Their profit could be used to purchase a more efficient automobile, making travel more efficient and thus saving more money. A family's profit could be used for investment in businesses. But taxation and inflation make saving difficult for the family. Profit is the lever upon which all economic growth depends. Whether for a family or a business enterprise, it is profit that makes growth possible.

In every endeavor one takes up, from reading Scripture to buying a new television, one expects to experience a net gain, whether it be monetary, spiritual, or intellectual. You picked up this book expecting to gain, or profit, from it. Profit in all its various forms is the basis of all human action.

Profit is the basis for all commerce. In any voluntary exchange, all participants profit. Historically, profit was thought to be a zero-sum interaction: that is, anything gained by one would be lost by another. But a careful examination of commerce shows this to be a fallacy.

Suppose one boy would not be willing to trade his Willie Mays baseball card for less than one dollar. We can say he values that card at one dollar. Suppose also that this boy loves bubblegum and would part with $1.50 for a hundred pieces. Another boy would pay $1.50 for a Willie Mays baseball card, but cares little for his hundred pieces of bubblegum. He would give up his gum for a dollar. These boys meet and trade their goods. Before the transaction, there was two dollars' worth of value in the two boys' possessions. After the trade, there was three dollars' worth of value—each, in a sense, profiting fifty cents in value from the trade.

We have examined God's concern for man's material welfare. The promises of prosperity in the Promised Land, Jesus' concern for the poor, and heavenly visions of gold-paved streets all show us that God is concerned with our material well-being as well as our spiritual well-being. We have seen that economics is an important and relevant field of study: we must look for the forces that will encourage and protect our prosperity. We have seen the relationship of four of these factors: production, tools, surplus capital, and profit. We have looked at some historical and present-day obstacles, such as the widespread but erroneous belief that tools cause unemployment, Marx's misguided theory on profit, and the taxation of profits. Understanding economic forces will help us to build a social order in agreement with God's plan and command to be stewards of the earth and to bear fruit.

49

FOUR
PROFIT IS NOT
A FOUR-LETTER WORD

The word *profit* today has a bad ring to it. It has become a six-letter obscenity. Just as "rugged individualism" has turned "individualism" into an ugly word, so also adjectives like "indecent," "exploitive," and "obscene" have given the word *profit* a bad taste. We bemoan the losses of major industries as their quarterly reports are summarized on newscasts. At the same time, we are filled with rage as we hear of the profits of large oil companies. We sympathize with the unfortunate but unproductive and inefficient producers who don't have the skills to meet public demand. We curse those who do meet demand and are rewarded for it. We view profit as a little chunk of the consumer taken cold-heartedly by the producer. Today, actual profits average less than five cents on the dollar. Yet public opinion polls show that the average American believes companies make thirty-five cents in profit from every dollar of sales revenue.

Profit performs an important role in the marketplace. It acts first as an incentive. Without hope of some kind of profit, there is no reason to work. Profit is a monetary pat on the back for a job well done. Profit is why we get up to go to work in the morning. With no hope of profit, Henry Ford would not have started the automobile industry. Necessity is not the mother of invention; profit is. Profit, as we saw in chapter 3, allows the accumulation of surplus capital needed for investment. Profit also acts as a gauge for future investment. If a producer is making large profits, it alerts investors that there is room for competition. Henry Ford's success led to the formation of competitors. Today, eighty years after the first Model T rolled off the line, there are over twenty-five car manufacturers worldwide. Had Ford not made a profit, not only would there be no competitors, but Ford himself would have moved on to producing something else. Lack of profits likewise alerts investors to stay out of a field which lacks significant demand. Profit is not a necessary evil, but rather an important cog in any free-market system. There is no set margin of legitimate profit margins, as prices come not through projected profits hopes but through the interaction of supply and demand.

To understand profit we must understand the nature of exchange. There are ultimately only two things which can be exchanged, goods and services. Money is not valuable in itself, but it has trade-in value for goods and services. Money is a promise for future goods or services. Exchanging goods or services directly, without using money, is called barter. Money makes the exchange indirect, as the money is later exchanged for goods and services. If I sell my car for money, I may spend that money later on a motorcycle. In effect I have bartered a car for a motorcycle. In this exchange, I value the money (or its purchasing power) more than the car. That is profit. The buyer of my car values the car more than the money. That is profit. All voluntary exchanges therefore end in mutual profit. Any coercive transaction is not true trade, but theft. Should the government wish to build a highway through my yard, whatever my reimbursement, that is an act of theft. Freedom is the key to profit, as only voluntary exchange insures *mutual profit.*

There is widespread confusion in our culture about the nature of profit. At a recent economics seminar a professor asked his audience the following question. "If a shoemaker spends forty dollars to make a pair of shoes and then goes to the marketplace and sells his shoes to a customer for fifty dollars, who makes the profit?" The vast majority of the audience gave the same answer, "the shoemaker." But in a business exchange that is entered into voluntarily this answer is only partially correct. The correct or full answer is "the shoemaker *and* the customer."

Trade and profit rest on the subjective nature of value. That is, no person can impose a value on something for him that he himself does not value. There is no *objective* value to a pair of shoes. In a bartering society exchange takes place something like this: The shoemaker produces fifty pairs of shoes. He has no need of fifty pairs of shoes, but he does need food. He has a *surplus* of shoes, but a scarcity of food. He prefers to eat steak, even if it tastes like shoe-leather, rather than to try to make his shoe-leather taste like steak. Meanwhile, back at the ranch, the cattle rancher has far more beef than he can possibly eat, but his toes are cold. He has a surplus of food, but a scarcity of shoes. He takes his beef to the shoemaker and makes a deal, exchanging his beef for shoes. In this transaction both trade one commodity for something else which, at the moment and in the particular circumstance, they value more highly. It is evident that in the exchange *both* profit. Both subjects get what they value more in exchange for what they value less.

In such a direct exchange, it is clear that both parties profit. If this were not so then the exchange simply would not take place. But something strange happens to our perception of things when the transaction takes place with the use of money. Money is an *indirect* means of exchange, more sophisticated and complex than the direct method of barter. Because of the indirectness of the exchange the mutual, reciprocal benefit of barter is obscured. The illusion is created that one party (the seller) profits, while the other party (the buyer) loses. In barter, it could be said that both parties are buyers and both parties are sellers. It is no different with indirect exchange. Behind the apparent legerdemain is the actual fact that the shoemaker sells his shoes to the customer in exchange for money and the customer "sells" his money to the shoemaker in exchange for shoes. Both sell. Both buy. Both profit.

The illusion of one-sided profit is enhanced by the public searchlight beamed on business profits. Businesses must report their profits and losses to the IRS, to their shareholders, to corporate boards, and so on. The individual must report all of his *income* to the government. He is not required to report all of his *purchases*. Yet, in reality, for both businesses and individuals, purchases are as much profit as wages.

A recent conference in Chicago featuring economists from the University of Chicago focused on economic problems of development in third-world countries. At one point, an agitated member of the audience complained that "the rich people are buying up all the land in India." The sentence hung in the air as a self-evident accusation of gross injustice going on in India, of the rich exploiting the poor. Then the speaker asked, "Is the land for sale in the marketplace?" The answer was yes. "Then, what is unjust about a rich man buying land that is offered for sale in a free transaction?" The acerbic cloud hovering over the original question was suddenly swept away.

But doesn't profit result from greed and the exploitive opportunism of one party taking advantage of another person's need? Isn't there something inherently dehumanizing about the marketplace? Greed is an ugly reality. No Christian can afford to neglect its devastating power of destruction. There are cases of exploitive opportunism such as selling a canteen of water to a person dying of thirst in the desert for a million dollars. But what Adam Smith so astutely understood was that the free market is the best check and balance system there is to curb the distortions of greed and exploitation. Greed cannot be profitable unless the greedy man's products are sold. In a free market the *customer* determines the price of the goods, not the greedy seller. If the customer doesn't want the greedy man's goods he simply won't buy them. If the greedy man succeeds, he will do so only if his greed indirectly benefits his customers by serving their needs or wants. If the greedy man seeks to profit exploitively by charging "too much" for his goods, the second Smithian plank of balance comes into play—competition. Even in the desert the exploiter can get his million dollars for a canteen of water only until someone else shows up and offers it for half the price. In a free market, competition forces the greedy to reduce prices or to go out of business.

Still we are left with the question of one person's taking advantage or profiting from another person's need. The maxim of free bartering or free market exchange is "From each according to his surplus, to each according to his wants." This could also be translated into "From each according to his surplus, to each according to his surplus." What lies behind this is the principle of division of labor. It assumes the social character of humanity. It assumes that no human being is ever totally self-sufficient. As God ordains things, there is a *diversity* as well as a *unity* to the human race. Just as in the church the eye cannot say to the ear, "I have no need of thee," in the marketplace the farmer cannot say to the shoemaker, "I have no need of thee." Rather than stifling co-humanity, a marketplace of voluntary exchange promotes it. What is dehumanizing is coercive collectivism where the state's power forces a kind of uniformitarianism that discourages individuality and the entrepreneurial spirit. Not only does history record the massive economic failures of collectivism, but it also indicates that where economic freedom is lost, political freedom perishes with it. In this system the inherent diversity of human gifts, vocations, and personalities is quenched. We envision hordes of Chinese people working at the same jobs, their vacant eyes peering at us over the enforced uniforms. The people dress the same way as a symbol of their enforced uniformitarian condition. In a free market I can wear plaid or tweed, blue jeans or three-piece suits. I can be a butcher, a baker, a candlestick maker at my discretion rather than at that of the coercive state.

Profit, in voluntary exchange, can never be obscene or exploitive. I may pay more than I want to pay for a given good or service, but I never pay more than I am willing. Should I pay ten dollars for a record which cost twenty-five cents to make, I am not being gouged or exploited. I am making a profit, for I value the record at more than ten dollars. Before we curse the business with which we make our exchanges, let us remember the nature of trade and mutual profit. Remember it is we who place value on the goods we purchase and on the goods we don't purchase. No one can make us buy anything we do not want (with the possible exception of the government). In a free market we buy what we want and thank those who produce what we want.

Many view prices as if they have come from an accounting wizard who figures costs, tacks on 10 or 20 percent, and sets the price. But prices are not determined by a producer's accountant, by a producer's president, by a producer's vice-president for consumer affairs, or by the custodian. Prices are determined by us, the buying public. The producers must sell a maximum number of units of a given good at a maximum price to attain maximum profit. Let us imagine that it costs Mr. Hershey twenty cents to make a candy bar. If he sold these bars for twenty dollars, he would likely profit nothing as few people would pay that much. If his candy bars cost twenty-one cents, he could sell perhaps a hundred thousand bars a day, profiting a thousand dollars a day. If these bars sold for twenty-five cents, and eighty thousand bars were sold per day, Hershey's profit would amount to four thousand dollars a day. The price that yields the highest profit is the price at which the producer will sell the product. The amount of profit rests solely on the amount people are willing to pay for any given object. When we see a twenty-five-cent candy bar on a counter, we must cast our economic vote. A yes vote means we exchange the quarter for the bar. A no vote, and the quarter remains firmly ensconced in pocket or purse.

The marketplace is not a place of totalitarian dictators; it is a democratic place where a dollar is a vote. In the end, majority rules. Perhaps our favorite automobile has been taken off the market because the dollar votes weren't there—not enough people bought the car. The consumer, the dollar-voting public, is the supreme ruler of the marketplace, able to bring out new products and get rid of old ones with the simple spending of a dollar. Producers do not produce junk and tell us to take it or leave it. Producers are suitors, vying for the attention of the spending public, aiming to please, to fulfill demands. Producers are not trying to just get by, or they will get no customers twice and go belly-up. The producer understands that he must please the consumer more than his closest competitor does. When it hurts to buy something, we must remember it's simply our indecision in the voting process and not the fault of the producer. If prices get to us, we should curse the consumers who pay them, not the producers who simply respond to their value system.

What should we do if prices for commodities we really need are higher than we want to pay? Rather than not buying and doing without, should we turn to government to bring the prices down? Governments have frequently interfered with the market price. Almost never has this interference produced a net gain for a given country. Price-fixing has never produced anything but hardship because it takes the consumer out of his rightful position as ruler of the marketplace and puts in his place the menace of Big Brother. Price-fixing doesn't fix anything; it only creates problems.

Economists speak of the *market price* for a given good. The market price is the price when there is no government interference. Let us use the candy bar to illustrate. The assumption is that the market price for all candy bars is twenty-five cents. The government fears that at this price the poor would have to live without the candy bar, something so American that it would be unpatriotic to deny it to anyone. The president announces on national TV that to avert the un-American distribution of candy bars, he has signed into law a bill requiring that all candy bars be sold for fifteen cents or less. This is called a *price ceiling*. We can expect one thing to happen immediately—candy bars will sell out. Rich, poor, Republican, Democrat, everyone will enjoy that great American delicacy, the candy bar. But the following day, there will be no candy bars. None. Why would anyone produce candy bars at a five-cent loss? No one would, and we'd be left with nothing to munch on. The government's plan to allow all to enjoy the candy bar results in no one's enjoying the candy bar. The net result of any price ceiling is always shortage. Government price ceilings on gasoline caused lines to grow to enormous lengths, while production went down. Why drill a new oil well when one can't make any profit on it? Price controls take the incentive out of investment and cause great shortages. No profit, no investment, no tools, no production, no wealth. Price ceilings designed to help the poor only hurt them and everyone else as well. History has proven this again and again. The market price allows for the best distribution, as those who want things the most pay for them. Those that do not care are not hurt.

Government price-fixing also comes in the form of price floors. These are designed to keep people producing "necessary" goods. The farming industry is heavily influenced by various price floor schemes today. Price floors are government-induced (forced) prices which are artificially above the real market price. Let us assume that the market price for a bushel of wheat in any given season is two dollars. The government, in order to protect the farmer (and win his voting support) will make any price below three dollars a bushel illegal. This is a price floor. As a result, thousands of young people, seeing farming now as an area of great profit, will head for the great outdoors to start their farms. Production will skyrocket, sales will plunge. The result is an enormous surplus. Tons of grain will (and do) slowly rot in elevators throughout our country. Soon the government will step in to correct the problem it created by promising to buy up all wheat which can't be sold. As a result, the farmer celebrates while the budget and the tax rates grow, along with the wheat.

Government schemes to affect prices have always been with us. The bad side effects of such policies remain with us also. But the real price, the consumer price, can always be found somewhere. If the price of a commodity is artificially controlled, the black market is where freedom truly reigns. There, one can find a candy bar despite the shortage. The black market is the free market in that it is beyond the power of taxation, price controls and regulation. The market price will always prevail whether it be in the open market or in a back alley. Government can pick at and harass the marketplace, but it cannot destroy it as long as people can produce and can place value on goods and services. Governments rise and governments fall, but the free market always survives.

But, everything I have said notwithstanding, there are instances when supply and demand must be put aside in Christian charity. Our man crossing the Sahara may fall at our feet, fighting dehydration, desperately in need of water. The demand for water is enormous, and this man would undoubtedly trade everything he owns for a glass of water. We happen to have a gallon of water in our tent. Although water is generally a common resource, in this circumstance we own a monopoly on this life-saving good. It is possible for us to exploit this situation for enormous material gain. But we are called to give freely to this desperate, man rather than to exploit him. This is not to say that supply and demand are evils in themselves. Supply and demand, when left alone, allow for the most equitable distribution of resources.

It should be noted that we are not here advocating government control of necessary utilities. In most areas around the country, the local or state government offers a monopoly to a utility company in exchange for the right to control it. This monopoly is unnatural, as it forbids competitors from entering the marketplace. Public utilities are controlled by government: they are run inefficiently, and they cost a great deal. Competition would bring prices down and quality up. It would disallow monopolistic prices and allow supply and demand to work as it ought, to everyone's advantage.

Governments have been exploiting people since the time of Amos, the poor man's prophet. Amos chastised Israel for their exploitive practices and promised the coming judgment of God. Amos 2:6 reads, "Thus saith the LORD; For three transgressions of Israel, and for four, I will not turn away the punishment thereof; because they sold the righteous for silver, and the poor for a pair of shoes." Selling the righteous for silver refers to the practice of unscrupulous judges receiving bribes, the act of declaring the innocent guilty for monetary reward. Selling the poor for a pair of shoes is Israel's second indictment. The Jewish nation had no bankruptcy laws; all debts were paid in full. If one man could not pay what he owed another, he would temporarily become the slave of the one he owed. This was not practiced to cause humiliation, but rather to be certain that all debts were paid. The debtor was taken to the judges at the gate of the city, and they would assess his value as a laborer. Judges often attributed absurdly low values, the price of a pair of shoes, to the labor of the debtors. This enabled the creditor to squeeze out as much labor from the debtor as possible. The debtor was robbed of his labor by the low value attributed to him.

These practices and others brought God's judgment down on Israel. These governmental practices hurt the poor man most. He could not find justice in the gates of the cities of Israel, God's chosen nation.

There are only two ways of acquiring what could realistically be called obscene profit: fraud and coercion. Obscenity is not the result of a high percentage of profit, but of dishonesty. The government's role in the economy is to prevent fraud and coercion. One must remember that Old Testament Israel, the only nation with its constitution and law written by God, had no bureaucratic agencies to regulate and interfere in the market. Old Testament government's involvement in the market was limited to stopping fraud and coercion.

The most common kind of fraud mentioned in the Old Testament was the use of false weights and measures. When buying, a merchant could obtain more than he paid for by using a false weight. When selling, he could cheat by using a weight which would measure out less than the customer paid for. Deuteronomy 25:13–16 reads:

> Thou shalt not have in thy bag divers weights, a great and a small. Thou shalt not have in thine house divers measures, a great and a small. But thou shalt have a perfect and just weight, a perfect and just measure shalt thou have: that thy days may be lengthened in the land which the LORD thy God giveth thee. For all that do such things, and all that do unrighteously, are an abomination unto the LORD thy God.

Leviticus 19:35–37 likewise forbids the use of false weights and measures.

Obviously we also are called to be honest. A twelve-ounce bottle of Coke must contain twelve ounces. A gallon of gas must be a gallon. A day's work must likewise be a day's work and nothing less. Illicit profit through fraud has been with us ever since the serpent promised Eve that the forbidden fruit would make her like God. The magic potions and healing elixirs of a traveling show are examples of fraud that deserves punishment.

Coercion is a more obvious form of illicit profit. Coercion comes in the form of theft, extortion, robbery, and often taxation. The thug trades protection (from himself) for money. He profits through the threat of violence or death. We do not enter the social security scheme voluntarily, but through coercion. We are offered, in a most humanitarian way, freedom from want in our old age. In the meantime, we are taxed, our children are taxed, our neighbors are taxed, and our parents are taxed, while legions of bureaucrats and politicians profit illicitly.

Force and fraud are two evils that have no place in the free market. They are subtle forms of slavery that rob the victim of the fruit of his labor. The Scriptures deplore these evils and implore government authorities to fulfill their proper role in stopping them. Whether they come in the form of a finger on the meat scale or a gun at our back, they are violations of the God-given right to private property.

Only two groups are capable of effecting coercive exchanges of goods and services: criminals and governments. The only essential difference between the two is a matter of legality. While it is illegal for the robber to steal my property at gunpoint, it is legal for the government to do it. This is seen most clearly in the principle of *eminent domain*. The dictionary defines the right of eminent domain as "the power of a government over all the property within its limits, by which it is entitled to appropriate, or to authorize the appropriation of, private property for public use, giving just compensation to the owner."

The problem with the principle of eminent domain lies in the last clause of its definition, "giving *just* compensation to the owner." Here, the theory goes, property is not stolen as in common theft. It is purchased at a "just" price. Nevertheless, it remains a coercive exchange, "justified" by its being for the common good. The issue is this: It is never, never, never possible to transact a just coercive exchange. Why not? In a coercive exchange the owner is *always* forced to sell his property at a lower value than he puts on it. Remember the subjective basis of value. There may be a going market price for land, but that does not affect the value a person puts on his own property. It provides him with a barometer of the value others may put on his property if he chooses to sell it, but in a free market his decision to sell or not to sell remains his. If the government offers to buy his land and he desires to sell it at the offered price, then the compensation is just. But if he is forced at gunpoint to sell when he does not desire to sell, he has been coerced into parting with his property at a price less than the value the property has for him. Thus, a coercive sale can never be just. If the government offers the man ten times the market value but the man values his land at eleven times the market value, the man has been robbed. Eminent domain is the government's legal license to steal. If the property owner resists the attempt of the armed robber to steal his goods, he is a hero. If he resists the government's coercive seizure of his land, which comes at the points of guns far more sophisticated and far more potent than those used by the common burglar, he is a criminal.

The infamous Old Testament King Ahab indulged in the use of eminent domain of sorts:

> Naboth the Jezreelite had a vineyard, which was in Jezreel, hard by the palace of Ahab king of Samaria. And Ahab spake unto Naboth, saying, Give me thy vineyard, that I may have it for a garden of herbs, because it is near unto my house: and I will give thee for it a better vineyard than it; or, if it seem good to thee, I will give thee the worth of it in money. And Naboth said to Ahab, The LORD forbid it me, that I should give the inheritance of my fathers unto thee. [1 Kings 21:1–3]

When Ahab reported Naboth's refusal to his wife, Jezebel, she replied with obvious sarcasm, "Do you now govern Israel?" Jezebel conspired to bring false charges against Naboth in the courts, and Naboth was summarily executed. We read: "And it came to pass, when Ahab heard that Naboth was dead, that Ahab rose up to go down to the vineyard of Naboth the Jezreelite, to take possession of it."

Ahab acquired the vineyard, but in the deed he received also the curse of God. Elijah pronounced God's judgment: "Thus saith the LORD, Hast thou killed, and also taken possession? . . . In the place where dogs licked the blood of Naboth shall dogs lick thy blood, even thine" (1 Kings 21:1–3, 16, 19).

The parallels of Ahab's action with the principle of eminent domain are evident. On the surface, however, there appear to be some significant differences. The appropriation of Naboth's land was for private gain to the king, not for the public good. Second, Naboth was executed on false charges rather than punished for violating the law.

The king did seek private, personal gain, but his act was not strictly a private matter. In a monarchy the king is a *persona publica*. In his office he embodies the public. In a sense the gain of the king is construed as a public gain. Here the clear distinction between private good and public good is obscured.

That Naboth was executed on *false* charges is also significant. It indicates that Israel did not have a law of eminent domain that could serve Ahab's interests. He tried to purchase Naboth's vineyard. When Naboth was unwilling to sell, Ahab had no authority to confiscate his property. The story tells of the abuse of government power, which provoked the unmitigated wrath of God.

Since God first promised Adam and Eve paradise in Eden in exchange for their obedience, our God has been making and keeping covenants. From Adam to Noah and his rainbow covenant, to Abraham and the covenant of salvation, God has faithfully kept his promises despite the disobedience of his people. Our God is not a fraudulent God; he is a covenant maker and keeper. The covenant principle is a simple one. One party promises something in exchange for the promise of the second party. Various penalties are to be made in the event of the violation of the covenant. The prophets from Elijah to Malachi warned the Jewish people of the coming sanctions for the violation of the covenant.

The covenant principle still operates today, not only in a religious sense, but in the marketplace as well. The modern-day contract is a covenant. Contracts are like covenant promises to fulfill a given task in exchange for another task. Labor–management negotiations are a hammering out of a covenant.

A contract is our assurance that there will be no fraud, that we will get what we pay for. Yet our culture reflects a society where covenants are easily broken. A wildcat strike, for example, is a violation of the covenant, or contract. The marriage contract is maintained only about 50 percent of the time; almost one in two marriages ends in divorce. Contract breaking is a violation of the ninth commandment, a form of fraud. Christ's words echo the ninth commandment, "Let your communication be, Yea, yea; Nay, nay: for whatsoever is more than these cometh of evil" (Mt. 5:37).

Profit is regarded by critics of a free market as an evil. They assume that profit necessarily results from oppression or exploitation of the worker. Karl Marx complained that profit alienates the worker from his labor. It is the owner who profits, not the worker. The owner gets rich at the expense of the laborer. This issue was brought up in the strike of the National Football League's Players' Union that forced an abbreviated season in 1982.

One of the heated issues in the strike centered on distribution of revenues earned from television. The players wanted a piece of the action, participation in ownership. Their argument was simple: they were the performers; they were the gate attraction that brought in the revenue. Without them there could be no profit. In addition they were the ones risking injury to their limbs while the owners enjoyed the comfort and safety of being spectators.

The argument touched on a complex array of economic and moral questions. The owners argued from an economic platform, saying that (1) the players were salaried employees working under contracts they had agreed on; (2) labor has no intrinsic right to profits above and beyond their salaries; (3) labor's market value is determined not by effort, but by supply and demand; (4) the players did not participate in the capital *risk* of the endeavor and should therefore not demand a portion of the capital gains of the enterprise.

The issue of the value of labor is crucial to the debate. In the marketplace, labor is a commodity, bought and sold just like goods and services. We might wish that people attached more value to our labor than they do. Indeed we may argue that they should do so. But these considerations have little effect on the marketplace, where the law of supply and demand reigns supreme. If there is a glut of schoolteachers, the value of the job decreases. If there is a scarcity of schoolteachers, their value increases, provided, of course, that there are people who want education. The same is true of football players. The players' argument that they are the ones people pay to see must be balanced by the fact that there are thousands of aspiring football players who would love to take their places. There is competition for their jobs. To be sure, they have secured their roster positions by convincing the owners that they are the best available performers and that their replacements would lower the quality of the team performance the public pays to watch. This is what gives the players their bargaining power.

On the other hand, the owners must know at what point it becomes unprofitable for them to give the public the best possible product. They may be induced to provide lesser thrills for lesser labor costs if their profit margin declines. The issue of the emergence of a competitive league, the U.S.F.L., adds to the competition and the complexity of the problem.

Professional football is called "professional" because it involves athletes who are paid to perform. They are not all paid the same amount because differences of positions and in skill affect the value of a player to the team. At a men's prayer breakfast at Willow Creek Community Church near Chicago, all-pro defensive back for the Chicago Bears, Doug Plank, related the following anecdote: When he reported to training camp he was amazed to discover he was being paid for what he loved to do for fun. But he wasn't in the league long until he learned that his employers wanted something in exchange for his pay. At the end of the season the Bears were winning a game against San Francisco when O. J. Simpson made a long run to beat them in the closing seconds. He broke six tackles on the way to the end zone. Plank was playing safety, so the last tackle Simpson broke was his. As safetyman, Doug was the last line of defense. As he started off the field he could see the fury gleaming in his coach's eyes. He screamed at him, "Plank! We're paying you $65,000 to make that tackle!" Doug looked the coach in the eye and said, "I know, Coach, but San Francisco is paying O. J. $800,000 to break that tackle."

Football is a business. Salaries are determined by the value of the individual to the company. When O. J. Simpson's knees were too weak to break tackles, his market value as a football player declined.

Salaries in a free market are determined by a business transaction that is a form of trade. The services of the individual are sold to the company at a price agreed upon by both parties. If it is a free transaction, no one is exploited. Marx failed to understand this when he complained that a wage earner is a kind of slave. To be sure, there is usually more money to be made in ownership than in wages, but there is also more to be lost. The salaried employee trades a degree of freedom for a degree of job security. The difference between a slave and a free wage earner is this: In a free market the worker is free to do the kind of work he chooses, to seek employment with the kind of company he prefers, to live where he chooses, and to quit his job if he chooses. In slavery the worker's work is selected for him; his wages are non-negotiable; his employer is selected for him; where he lives is determined for him; he is not allowed to quit. In a word, he is *owned*.

The risk factor of the owner is often overlooked, especially when it is the successful owner who receives so much attention in the public eye. Consider the story of Art Rooney. He invested his private capital in the Pittsburgh Steelers. For forty years Rooney's team never won a division championship. The ledger book of his company was literally sprinkled with red ink. The fans stayed away from football games while screaming their frustrated slogan, "S.O.S." ("Same Old Steelers"). Then came the seventies and four Super Bowl championships. Suddenly Rooney owned a bonanza. Season tickets sold out years in advance. Suddenly the present crop of players who risked none of their capital over that forty-year span wanted a piece of the ownership. Rooney was not disposed to give it to them. He recalled vividly the absence of players clamoring to participate in his losses during the lean years.

In summary, profit, at any rate, barring force and fraud, is not an evil. It is the result of the level of demand by consumers, and voluntary exchange. Government attempts to tamper with profits disturb the balance between supply and demand, creating surpluses, shortages, and injustices.

FIVE
WHAT MONEY CAN DO

The first free trade probably took place soon after the first instances of fraud and covenant breaking. Satan's great sale had taken place and Eden was an old memory to Adam and Eve. The earth was beginning to be populated. Men left their crude homes in search of the day's food, equipped only with an empty stomach and a few stones. One man stayed behind working on his new idea. He had seen a once ferocious lion virtually paralyzed by pain from a small thorn in his paw. The man found a sharp stone and lashed a small stick to it. He had designed the world's first spear, a jumbo thorn.

The following day, our ingenious young man left his cave early in the morning and returned in a short while, dragging a large deer with the monstrous thorn in its side. The other hunters returned later and gazed in wide-eyed wonder at their hermit-like friend beaming proudly beside his kill. The inventor slept well on a stomach filled with venison. The following day he was able to construct two of these newfangled spears. He gave them to two neighbors in exchange for a portion of their kill. Barter was born.

Barter is the exchange of goods or services for other goods or services. The first trade took place in barter form. The process of barter did much to alleviate economic misery. It also heralded the advent of division of labor. Some people produced weapons while others hunted. The newfound abundance of meat made possible by the technological breakthrough of the spear allowed others to leave hunting for businesses of their own. They produced animal skins or pottery, or they chopped firewood. Our first entrepreneur, of course, bartered only for traditional skins which were beyond the whims of fashion, a tradition which he passed on to future generations of his family. There were no spear control laws, no taxation of profits, no barter fixing to interfere with the wealth of these early men.

Barter flourished as its benefits became apparent. The hermit was able to invest his time into finding a sharper stone for constructing spears. The growth of the hunting industry gave the hunters greater purchasing power, and as a result, other industries grew as well. After the hunt everyone gathered to trade wares. Soon others joined the established industries and competition began. Hunters had to find the finest meats, makers of clothing had to find the softest and warmest skins, and woodcutters had to find the best-burning trees. Where once everyone huddled, hungry and cold, in damp dark caves, now they enjoyed the luxury of a filling meal, warm clothes, and a fire. All this resulted from the idea of one lonely man and the implementation of his idea. Barter had allowed the accumulation of these luxuries. It encouraged people to work harder and smarter. People began to look for better tools and more efficient work habits.

Although barter was a great breakthrough in the production of wealth, its power and scope were limited. One could trade only when two people were in need of each other's product. One had to find someone who not only wanted what the first had, but also had what the first person wanted. The spearmaker grew tired of trading for meat. The hunters grew tired of trading for spears. Sometimes barter could be arranged through three parties. The skinmaker wanted meat, the hunter wanted a spear, and the spearmaker wanted a skin. The hunter traded his meat for a skin, then traded his skin for a spear. Everyone was happy, but the transaction took a great deal of time and energy. Besides, barter neared its limit in the three-way deal, as it was almost impossible to find four or more producers with compatible interests and the time or desire to arrange such a complicated deal.

The hermit, the great economic thinker of his community,

searched long and hard for a solution. After many sleepless nights it dawned on him. He entered the market the following day armed with a bundle of high quality spears and an armful of clay tablets. The tablets bore this inscription: "The holder of this tablet may redeem it for one spear." A frustrated skinmaker approached the hermit, bemoaning the limits of their barter system. The hermit, whose skins were threadbare, offered a tablet to the skinmaker. The skinmaker explained that he had no need for a spear at the present time. The hermit explained that someone undoubtedly would in the near future, someone who perhaps had something the skinmaker would want. The two made a deal. The skinmaker traded a skin for a tablet, which he redeemed for a small bear (skin intact) before the day was done.

The hermit's new idea did not take hold instantly, but eventually all producers installed tablets into their market proceedings. Thus money began. Trade once again boomed beyond anyone's wildest imagination. A shoemaker, a butcher, and a water gatherer started new businesses. These men prospered. The tablets were used more and more as the community reached a new height in prosperity. Trade was no longer restricted to two or three people. Tablets could now reach each producer before being exchanged for their real worth.

Then once more growth leveled off and the community reached a new plateau. The problem was apparent to everyone. Each person valued his products differently. If the skinmaker wanted only a pound of meat he didn't want to trade a full skin or the right to a spear. The community turned its eyes to the hermit who had grown old and wealthy since his original spear venture. Again he suffered through long nights racking his brain for a solution. The problem was that tablets were difficult to cut into halves or fourths. Unless it was whole, it was worthless. Then suddenly he saw the answer. Rather than tablets, he would find something divisible, something anyone could see. The next day at the market he put up a sign at his booth: "Spears For Sale, One Tablet or Fifteen Beads." Soon all trade was done in beads. Seven beads for a pound of deer, twenty-five beads for a new skin. Trade boomed once more, and the community thanked their genius hermit, who retired to write down his findings and discoveries for other communities around the world.

Beads were one of the earliest forms of money. Other products such as shells, rocks, sticks, skins, and feathers were used as well. These products were of little use in themselves. The value of money lies in its acceptance as an indirect medium of exchange. The power of money is that it can be traded; it can be exchanged for goods and services. Money is the go-between, the middleman in the exchange of goods and services. To have any value, money must be acceptable in exchange for goods and services. If the skinmaker left his community, no matter how many beads he took with him, he might not be a rich man. In another community, shells, not beads, might be the medium of exchange. If the skinmaker wanted meat, but the hunter was unwilling to accept the beads, the skinmaker was a pauper. His beads were useless.

To understand what money is, we must first examine what money is not. Money is not wealth. Money cannot feed, shelter, or clothe man. By itself, money cannot give physical comfort to anyone. Imagine yourself on a desert island. After your ship sank, you managed to reach this tropical island with the clothes on your back and a suitcase full of neatly piled hundred-dollar bills. You cannot eat the money; you cannot shelter yourself with it; and you cannot clothe yourself with it. You cannot buy protection from lions and tigers and bears; you cannot buy a return ticket home with it. You are left with a suitcase full of daydreams of what might have been. Robinson Crusoe, on another nearby island, is penniless but enjoys wealth (food, clothing, and shelter) that will take you years to accumulate as you produce the bare necessities of life. Wealth lies in production, not in beads, shells, rocks, paper, or gold.

Money is not a fixed measure of quantity or quality. The five thousand dollar automobile of 1910 was greatly inferior to the two thousand dollar automobile of 1952. The ten thousand dollar house of 1910 was greatly superior to the ten thousand dollar house of 1947. In 1932 a dollar bought five times as much wheat as it did in 1952. The same dollar that represented a hundred pieces of gum to you as a child represents fifty pieces of gum today.

If a bottle containing fifty pieces of bubblegum were to wash up

on the beaches of Robinson Crusoe's island, you could not purchase
the gum with all the money in your suitcase. The money would be
as useless to Mr. Crusoe as it is to you. You cannot look at your
dollar and declare that it is worth fifty pieces of gum. Tomorrow it
could be worth five hundred pieces, or ten. Tomorrow the gum
could be of such quality that you would exchange your dollar for
one piece of gum, or perhaps you would want no gum at all. In a
standard economy, one with a stable money supply, the fluctuations
in purchasing power are due to the new goods produced. Money,
even under the gold standard, is not altogether stable in its purchasing power from one time to another.

Money is not always pieces of paper or metal. Historically money
has taken many forms. Today most of the money in circulation is
bank credit, seen only in the form of bank checks. Money flows
easily through computers, making the cumbersome process of cash
transfer less common and less necessary.

Money is not a *claim* against goods or services, nor are goods
and services a *claim* against money. The exchange depends upon
the *willingness* of the owners of particular goods and services to
trade with the owners of money. Money claims nothing, but it can
be traded for goods and services under any situation of mutual
consent.

Money is not wealth; it is not a fixed quantity or quality; it has
no fixed future value in terms of goods or services; it is not always
pieces of paper or metal; and it is not a claim against goods or
services. Money is a medium of exchange for goods and services.
The recipient of the money then trades it for other items, *ad infin-
itum.*

As long as the money supply remains stable, the power of money
remains relatively stable, no matter how many times it has exchanged hands. (The effects of an unstable money supply on this
system will be examined in the following chapter.) Money is like
the power of a river stream that can drive any number of millwheels.
The power is not affected by the number of the people through
whose hands it flows. Money, whether beads or gold, acts as a
catalyst to trade in the marketplace, allowing more transactions to
take place. As we examine the mutual profit in all voluntary ex-

changes, we see that money, the catalyst, adds to our nation's wealth, not in itself, but by allowing more transactions to take place and therefore to increase profit.

Money changed its form with the passing of time. When man began to cultivate soil and to tame animals, commodities such as grain and oil, dried fish, tortoise and cowry shells, sheep, horses, and especially cattle were used as mediums of exchange. The ox, which was one of the most marketable of all available goods, was a popular medium of exchange in the ancient world. It was used by ancient Greeks, Hebrews, Romans, Arabs, and many other people up to the late Middle Ages. As the division of labor spread, urban development began around the world. Cattle money was slowly phased out in favor of metals then in use. With the advent of metal handicrafts, copper, bronze, gold, and silver became the most widely accepted form of money. Precious metals were first used as money in their finished forms of weapons and ornaments. When these metals became more widely recognized, they began to be used as raw materials rather than as finished goods. As trade over the known world grew, so did the acceptance of these precious metals. Gold, silver, bronze, and copper became the money of civilized people. Precious metals were extremely useful in the marketplace, making trade less cumbersome. They were accepted worldwide, and they could be easily divided. Precious metals could be transported at a low cost, allowing the expansion of trade over large areas of land. The metals could also be stored with relative safety. Many of the earlier mediums of exchange, such as grain and meat, were perishable and therefore could not be stored for long.

There remained one serious inconvenience with the use of metals in the marketplace. Each transaction required constant testing and weighing of the metals. To solve this problem the Lydians of Asia Minor in 650 B.C., and soon thereafter the Greeks, began to use coins. Coins were small pieces of metal with a visible mark of guarantee for their weight and fineness. Paul Einzig, author of *Primitive Money*, proposes that coinage may have been invented during the late Mycenaean period from 1400 to 1100 B.C. This coinage system is believed to have perished with the Mycenaean civilization.[3] George MacDonald, author of *Evolution of Coinage*, believes that coins were used in China long before they were used in Asia Minor, during the eleventh century B.C. or even earlier. Whatever the case, precious metals have been made into coins continuously from 650 B.C. Early coins were made of a natural mixture of gold and silver. Later coins used bronze, copper, pure gold, and silver. These early coins carried a variety of symbols and portraits. We recall the attempt of the scribes and chief priests to trap Jesus. They asked Jesus,

> Is it lawful for us to give tribute unto Caesar, or no? But he perceived their craftiness, and said unto them, . . . Shew me a penny. Whose image and superscription hath it? They answered and said, Caesar's. And he said unto them, Render therefore unto Caesar the things which be Caesar's, and unto God the things which be God's. [Luke 20:22–25]

The Roman coin of the early first century bore the face of Caesar. This coin, following the Roman armies, was used in trade throughout the empire at the time of Christ. Coins became the most popular medium of exchange all over the world and constituted universal money until the beginning of the twentieth century. Trade prospered as barriers separating coinage systems were broken down. As trade prospered, so also did the material welfare of those involved in the trade. Profit possibilities were magnified enormously as trade moved from the first few producers in the hunting community to the entire world.

As trade grew, coins changed dramatically. Any metal used in trade must maintain a delicate balance of scarcity and plenty. If a metal is too common, its value is eroded and it fades out of the trading process. If a metal is too scarce, it soon loses its acceptability and must also fade out of the trading process. Copper, being too common, dropped out as a major medium of exchange. Bronze later dropped out for the same reason. Soon, silver and gold became the universal means of exchange.

For twenty-five hundred years, hard money—money from precious metals—has been the market medium of exchange. This was the case up to the first half of the twentieth century. The coinage of gold began in 650 B.C. Coins were manufactured both by private and public mints. The oldest coins were probably issued privately to meet the requirements of markets or firms. The governments, seeing this as an area of possible profit, joined in the manufacturing of these coins. The governments were successful in this endeavor, but their success was limited by the competition of private mints. To remove this barricade to profit, governments began to outlaw the private manufacture of coins used in trade. Governments created for themselves monetary monopolies.

In the contemporary situation, governments around the world are the sole coiners of money. The proposition that private companies could coin money is so foreign to modern man that it is often thought to be an economic impossibility. Yet few governments in history have been able to resist the temptation to use their legal power over money to their own advantage. From early history rulers have been known to "clip" their coins. Later governments put holes in the centers of their coins, claiming it necessary for identification. These actions served to devaluate the coins and cast a shadow over their integrity. But the coin system survived these petty abuses. Trade continued to flourish. The coin enabled trade to spread across the world.

The coin was universally held in high esteem. As the glory of gold spread, nations began to value gold more than what it could purchase. This led to the fallacy of *mercantilism*. Mercantilism arose as an economic movement in Europe in the eighteenth century based on the premise that a country should attempt to sell more than it buys in order to accumulate gold. The fact that useful goods and services constitute real wealth was obscured. Nations began to try to produce and sell all over the world, but to *buy* only at home, storing up gold and silver. The fallacy of this system is quite apparent. Gold is not of great use apart from trading. Nations can use only so much gold for weaponry and ornaments. Nations that accumulated gold could enjoy its shiny splendor. Nations that traded, that bought goods with gold, enjoyed the products that they purchased.

Money is not wealth, whether it be paper money or hard money. Wealth is goods and services. Gold's primary value was in that it could be traded for any goods around the world. Sitting gold, gold not being used as a medium of exchange, is basically useless. Sitting gold is like a stream that has been redirected around the millwheels to build a pool of water. The pool is nice to look at, but it won't help you produce.

America is in an uproar over foreign competition. American industries resort to the myths of mercantilism by running to the government and asking for protection from Japanese competitors who sell their goods within our borders. President Reagan, for example, raised the import duty on foreign motorcycles to protect America's sole producer, Harley-Davidson. America is fearful because we are not selling outside the country and buying inside the country. Americans are caught up in the counterproductive game of mercantilism, and we are losing.

News commentators periodically report to us the latest figures on trade deficits. Trade deficits are a contradiction in terms in a free market. We have already shown that mutual profit is the result of every trade transaction. Imagine a sportscaster reading the score of a baseball game between Japanese and American all-stars, "America lost its game with the Japanese today by a score of 5–5." The idea of trade deficits violates the law of noncontradiction. Trade, by definition, is equal and can contain no deficits. Imagine John Q. Public of Middletown, USA, buying a car from Toyota of Japan. This "unpatriotic" man has just caused a man in Detroit to lose his job. That is trade deficit, something to be avoided. What can Toyota do with its new American dollars? It can do only two things with them—put them in its vault and look at them, or spend them. Looking at paper dollars hasn't the same thrill as looking at gold. If that money remains in the vault, America has one more car, and Japan has more paper. The only other option is that the car dealer spend the money. American dollars, any nation's dollars, will all ultimately be spent in the nation that produced them. The money comes back to America, and some goods or services go to Japan. There is no deficit because trade, whether through barter or indirectly through money, is always equal and must be so. Import tariffs do not save American jobs, they merely save the jobs of inefficient producers at the expense of efficient producers who produce that which other countries want. Mercantilism, though long since refuted in Adam Smith's *Wealth of Nations*, is flourishing as an economic system even though people cannot flourish because of it.

Mercantilism, though a strong and destructive force, did not stop trade and the use of gold as the medium of exchange altogether. However, gold eventually gave way to paper as the medium of exchange. The paper, like our first country's tablets, could be exchanged for gold. Paper seems an odd form of exchange for gold. Gold, having scarcity and being in demand, has market value. Paper, on the other hand, is plentiful and renewable. Nevertheless, it has come to be used as the medium of exchange in the market. Paper is more portable than gold, and easier to use. Why did people accept paper rather than hard money? The reasons for a change from gold to paper are relatively simple.

Imagine yourself as a baker working hundreds of years ago. You have within your house one hundred units of gold. This gold is open to theft. You, wanting to keep your gold safe, deposit it in a warehouse. The warehouse owner gives you a receipt for your gold. Your neighbor, the butcher, puts a hundred units of his own gold in the same warehouse and receives his receipt. The butcher wishes to buy a loaf of bread from you at a cost of one unit of gold. The butcher could walk to the warehouse, ask the owner for a unit of gold, walk back to the baker, and pay his one unit of gold. This, of course, is an extremely inefficient way of doing business. An exchange of receipts, a receipt for one piece of gold for one loaf of bread, could take place within the bakery without the wasteful walking back and forth. This was how paper money began to be used in the marketplace. Paper money, these certificates of deposit, circulate through the economy. The baker may approach the shoemaker with the butcher's receipt and nine of his own and exchange them for a pair of shoes. These certificates can circulate endlessly. Always, however, behind the paper, is a promise: the paper can be exchanged for its corresponding gold value. The acceptance of paper lay in the fact that it could be, at any time, exchanged for a scarce commodity, for gold.

If Rip Van Winkle had gone to sleep in 1963 with a fistful of dollars, he would have had in his hands a promise that they could be exchanged for silver. The U.S. dollar in 1963 could be redeemed at any time for silver. If Rip woke up today and headed to his bank with his old and wrinkled dollars, he would receive only a puzzled look when he asked for silver in exchange. Today, our money bears the promise of *nothing*. Paper money is no longer a certificate of deposit of anything; it has no hard value behind it. If Rip were owed thirty silver dollars at the time of his nap, he would now have to accept the payment of his debt in paper dollars. What is behind paper money now is government force. All paper money in America today bears the words *legal tender*, meaning that debtors have the legal right to pay all debts in paper money. This system works within the borders where the government has the power to enforce its legal tender. Outside those borders the value of the paper fluctuates according to people's confidence in the promises of the government that issues the currency.

The specter of Gresham's Law contributes to the economic instability of many of the world's nations. The law, simply stated, declares that "bad money drives out good money." Good money tends to be hoarded rather than circulated. Try an experiment. Reach in your pocket for a quarter. Drop that quarter on a counter. How does it sound? Now pick it up and read the date on it. Is the coin dated before 1964? Surely it isn't. If it were, you would want to save it rather than spend it. Why? Because the silver content of the coin could be sold at more than its currency value. That is the simple reason that pre-1964 coins are no longer in circulation. If you own such a coin, continue the experiment by dropping it on a counter. Listen to its ring. Compare it to the dull thud of the coins of recent vintage. You will see why Gresham's Law works.

SIX
THE INFLATIONARY RIP-OFF

Imagine Gallup pollsters taking to the streets armed with paper and pads. They pose the question, "What is inflation?" Chances are that a sizable majority will answer, "Higher prices." This answer reflects a serious misconception fostered in part by a government campaign to take the heat off themselves and place it squarely on the back of the business community. One man explained the riddle of inflation to me in this manner. A butcher grows tired of owning only one automobile. To raise the money for a second car he raises his prices. The plumber, in order to afford the butcher's higher prices, likewise raises his prices. The mechanic, in order to pay his plumbing bill, raises his prices. This process continues throughout the community. But if this chain reaction occurred in a marketplace with a stable money supply, no one could buy anything. If the money supply remained the same while prices escalated, the money supply would not fit the number of available goods and services.

In a stable supply situation, the butcher who first raised his prices would lose his business to other butchers who were satisfied with one car. Remember that it is the consumer, not the producer, who sets the price in a free market. If the butcher wants a second car he must do his job more efficiently and provide for the consumer better than his nearest competitor. By raising prices merely to satisfy his own desires, he would quickly price himself out of business.

My grandfather often talks about prices when he was young. Fifty years ago, movies were a quarter, candy bars a nickel, and the best New York strip steaks were little more than a dollar at his favorite posh restaurant in downtown New York City. Things have changed dramatically. The rise in prices is not inflation; it is the *result* of inflation. Inflation is not the change from a five-cent candy bar to a thirty-cent candy bar. *Inflation is the increase in the money supply.* The quantity of money is inflated, resulting in a proportionate deflation of the unit value of the currency. Such a change in the money supply makes the jump in prices not only possible, but necessary. Government figures on inflation, the consumer price index, are not a measure of inflation, but a measure of the effects of inflation. The government covers its tracks by pointing to the producers, rather than by announcing its monthly increase in the money supply. Inflation comes from the government printing office, not from business. Government is the only possible source of inflation except for counterfeiters.

Imagine a tiny mythical country with only ten loaves of bread and nothing more. This country has within it ten units of currency and ten citizens. Each loaf of bread is equal in value to one unit of currency. A printing press is introduced into the country. This press cranks out ten more units of currency. Each loaf of bread is now worth two units of currency, as there are ten loaves and twenty units. The price has just doubled. The wealth of the country remains the same. There are twenty units, but still only ten loaves. The salaries of the ten citizens would, without a doubt, double. No one would be any richer, because production would remain the same. Wealth cannot be measured by the amount of currency one brings in, but rather by the goods and services which one can trade for.

Not too long ago, the American dollar could be exchanged for a given amount of gold. The American dollar was a receipt for gold, just as clay tablets were once redeemable in spears. Today's American dollar is redeemable in American dollars, and nothing else. Our dollar is backed by history, by a standard of the past, by 150 years of hard stable money. Our government gives us only currency, currency with no hard value, paper with nothing to stand behind it. "Gold bugs," economists calling for a return to hard money, are anachronisms, lonely prophets heard by few and heeded by still fewer.

Even the defenders of free enterprise, the renowned Chicago school led by Nobel Prize winner Milton Friedman, have renounced the gold standard, calling for limited inflation and a controlled level of fiat currency to "stimulate" a stagnated economy. When the money supply swells, paychecks swell and salaries enter higher and higher tax brackets. The gross national product seems to grow as well, if the effects of inflation are not taken into account. We wonder how our parents and their parents before them could live on their paltry incomes. But their "meager" incomes could be traded for gold. The incomes were in hard money, not paper money.

We have examined the futility of printing fiat money in our ten-loaf, ten-person, ten-unit mythical nation. The doubling of the currency proved to be useless, but harmless, folly. The effects of inflation on a nation, however, can be far more serious. The process that begins with production, produces surplus capital, and leads to material prosperity is damaged with the introduction of inflationary practices. If the money supply is doubled, the value of the money held before the doubling is cut in half. Let us suppose you are the proprietor of a very successful business. As you satisfy the demands of the buying public, profits pour in. In order to make your business more successful, you hope to invest in the latest machinery to produce your product. You diligently save your profits, but their value plummets as the government printing press increases the money supply. The value of your savings falls and falls.

It is folly to save in such an environment because the longer you save, the lower your money value plunges. If you earn 5 percent interest on your savings and the annual inflation rate is 10 percent, you have a net annual loss of 5 percent. You quickly pull your money out of the bank and spend it. Your reaction is integral to the Keynesian system designed to stimulate consumer spending. Consumer spending, you will remember, is essential to material prosperity. An increase in consumer spending due to inflation sends false messages to producers, leading many to believe that they need to expand. But this increase is due to the declining value of paper money, and not to increased wealth or production. The increased demand is an illusion.

As in the mythical ten-loaf town, the extra ten dollars didn't signify more production, just more paper. Had the bread factory assumed higher demand and stepped up production, a lot of bread would have gone stale. Factories are built and workers hired, but they fade away when the illusion is exposed. The early seventies were a time of expansion all over the country. Today we are paying for taking part in the illusion, as we have countless times before, after every period of inflation in our history.

Inflation brings pressure to spend, spend, spend. Saving is folly, both for the proprietor of a business and for any family. It doesn't take a genius to realize that if he's earning 5 percent interest at the bank, but inflation goes at a rate of 10 percent, he's losing money. Families cease to save, and a serious depletion of surplus capital occurs. As we have seen, if surplus or investment capital diminishes, investment in tools declines, production falls off, and the wealth of the nation falls.

Banks learn quickly also. If a bank lends money at a rate of 8 percent, and the inflation rate is at 10 percent, the bank is losing money. It receives its payment in devalued money. It's commonly believed that inflation means easy money for borrowing. Instead, inflation necessitates high interest rates to cover the loss of receiving devalued money. At the same time, individuals are taking their money out of banks and spending it. This causes a shortage of loanable funds resulting in still higher interest rates. With skyrocketing interest rates and inflationary incentives to spend and not save, investment in the tools of production plummets. The end result is a decrease in material prosperity.

Inflation eats away at the core of material prosperity, capital investment. It encourages consumer spending at the expense of consumer saving. Inflation is like encouraging someone to eat and then taking away the means of producing food. The rich are not buying jewels, yachts, furs, and works of art because they are stupid or greedy; they consume lavishly because these goods devalue more slowly than paper money in the bank. Do not blame the rich, blame the government that cannot practice the first law of "house-rule":

that of not spending more than comes in. Blame the government that believes consuming rather than producing is the key to prosperity. Blame the government that eats away at the savings of its citizens. Blame the government that sets itself above its own laws and the laws of God by practicing policies that must, and do, debase the people's currency.

The news reports tell us of budget deficits, federal reserve plans, appropriations, stopgap spending, and the consumer price index. One word is glaringly missing—*counterfeiting*. Yet the problem of inflation is precisely the problem of "legal counterfeiting."

Suppose that each year I write out a projected budget for the coming months. My annual income is $12,000. My annual expenditures amount to $14,000. I project a $2,000 deficit. In a dark, musty corner of my basement lies the solution to my problem: a printing press. Every night I quietly print crisp one-dollar bills to cover my deficit. These bills bear the words *legal tender*, and they are accepted everywhere I go. My budget now balances. My conscience is soothed by remembering that $2,000 in fake bills increases consumer spending and will help our ailing economy. The next year, due to inflationary pressures, my income is upped to $15,000, but my expenditures reach the $20,000 mark. I am forced to work longer hours in my damp corner to cover this $5,000 deficit, but I rejoice in stimulating the economy. One day two policemen come to my door toting guns, handcuffs, and a search warrant. I enter the police station handcuffed but smiling. I have no fear of imprisonment, because I have a precedent.

I arrive at my trial, trusting myself as my counsel, having taken a correspondence course in law. I stand to speak.

"Your honor, ladies and gentlemen of the jury, I stand before you an accused man. I am charged with counterfeiting. I stand guilty. Guilty of following in the noble tradition of the red, white, and blue, guilty of patriotism, guilty of helping our ailing economy. Send me to prison if you will, but send also our leaders of state, the counterfeiters for the cause of prosperity. Send also the citizens who elected our leaders to do this great deed of counterfeiting. Send the American nation to prison, for if I am guilty, we are all guilty. The defense rests."

I am terrified when the judge offers me ten years of rest in a federal prison, and I am relieved to awaken from this nightmare in a cold sweat. The problem with government counterfeiting is that it is not a dream, but a reality, continuing during the reigns of Republicans and Democrats, liberals and conservatives. The national debt grows like a deadly weed. Inflation is not just some small governmental error, but counterfeiting on a grand scale. For the private individual the practice of printing bogus, worthless paper and putting it in circulation is a criminal act. Yet it is legal for governments to do it. The practice of inflating the money supply with fiat currency is an act of national theft. Governments that face huge deficits resort to this measure to be able to pay their debts. It becomes an addiction. Withdrawal is called a depression, yet it is the only cure for a monetary system devalued by counterfeit money.

Despite all the subtle words and diversionary tactics, the reality of American counterfeiting cannot be denied. It is reflected in shrinking savings accounts, higher interest rates, lower capital investment, and higher prices. This is not the result of one greedy butcher, nor of a million greedy butchers, but rather of a government that wants to spend, but is afraid to increase taxes. The two primary means of income for the government are taxes and creating money out of thin air. The latter is merely a disguised form of taxation. Inflation costs the people dearly, but the costs are hidden, at least until the taxpayer sees the results of higher prices. But the tax-power of inflation is complex, and most citizens apparently do not understand the heavy costs that lie at the end of the inflationary maze.

In the 1980 election campaign, inflation was a central issue. Gerald Ford's WIN campaign didn't, and inflation reached double digits during the Carter administration. Double-digit inflation aroused the public though most did not fully understand the complexities of the issue. What people did understand was that the purchasing power of their dollar had shrunk. The pain in their pocketbooks produced a howl in the polling booth.

In a Gallup poll taken in 1983, only 5 percent of the people polled indicated that inflation was a concern for them in the next

presidential election. In the short space of three years, the problem
of inflation was solved. A miracle of Reaganomics! The inflation
rate dropped to between 3 and 4 percent. The new central issues
were high interest rates and severe unemployment. A clamor arose
for job programs, for government to provide funds for relief to those
suffering from unemployment. With an annual deficit approaching
$200 billion, the public cried for more government spending to
solve the present woes of unemployment.

Think. In Carter's administration the annual budget deficit
reached $50 billion for the first time in U.S. history. The deficit
was quadrupled in four years, an average of 100 percent per year.
Consider that the entire federal budget during the Johnson administration was considerably less than the present annual deficit.

We return to ask, what causes inflation? The proximate answer,
of course, is the monetary policies that allow the government to
print fiat currency. But why are governments induced to use such
practices? A deficit does not necessitate fiat currency. Printing
money is only one alternative. Other measures can be used to over-
come deficits: the government could reduce its spending, or it could
raise taxes. No law of causality says deficits *cause* inflation; other
alternatives do exist to meet the problem. But oh, the temptation
on public officials to roll the presses, in light of the other options.
Consider the politician's choice.

He can choose to cut federal spending. Imagine the national crises
that would follow a sudden reduction of government spending of
$200 billion. Masses of government employees would be out of
work. Entitlement and welfare programs would be seriously cur-
tailed. Private interest groups would be furious. Very possibly there
would be blood in the streets as those who suffered losses of government benefits rose up in angry revolt. Cutting spending means
losing votes. Our culture has introduced new phrases into our national vocabulary, phrases that are a daily litany on the lips of
elected officials. The phrases include "special interest groups" and
"We can't; it's an election year."

He can vote to increase taxes. Political historians argue that people become revolutionary if their taxes reach a certain level. That

level has already been doubled in the United States, and governments fear (rightly) that to meet the deficits by significant increases in taxes would be political suicide. They prefer policies of economic suicide to the political variety.

Or he can inflate the money supply. By increasing the money supply the government can gain certain advantages. First, it can pay its debts with devalued currency. (Debtors benefit from inflation, while creditors suffer.) Second, the government will receive more money in taxes because salaries will rise. The ratio of growth will not remain constant because of the phenomenon of "bracket creep": As people's salaries rise to match the rising prices that come from an inflated money supply, people will find themselves in a higher tax bracket. They will be required to pay more, proportionately, in taxes. This is one reason economists call inflation a "hidden tax." The disadvantage, politically, of inflationary monetary policies is that sooner or later they create a public furor. But this solution has an easy out, because the public is easily deceived. The printing presses can be turned on or off, depending on the public mood. It is relatively easy to manipulate inflation. As Milton Friedman has suggested, it only requires the pushing of a button to stop or start the presses.

Stop the presses and you get recession with unemployment. Start the presses and you get higher prices, a loss of investment capital, a decline in production, and failing businesses. The public will probably not understand what government manipulation is doing to the economy because there is a time lapse between inflating the money supply and reaping the dire economic consequences. If during the time lapse the machines are shut off, the inflation rate will drop. Then the nation lives out the later consequences of the earlier inflation. During the consequence period, the public looks at the visible branches and forgets the root. Suddenly unemployment becomes the issue, and inflation becomes a concern of only 5 percent of the population. The government responds by spending more money and enlarging the deficit to "meet the needs of the people." This, of course, increases the temptation to turn the presses on again for a new cycle. Such a policy is as effective as extinguishing fire by pouring gasoline on it. The real causes of economic woes are obscured by the pressures of the immediate. The urgent becomes a tyrant, inducing the politician to choose the expedient rather than the prudent, because the public demands it.

The Wall Street crash of 1929 was a frightening experience. Survivors of the Great Depression tell tales of living through it with the pride of those who landed on Omaha Beach on D-day. The economic upheaval was like none America had ever seen. There had been depressions before, all preceded by a period of inflation. These depressions came and went quickly, as the politicians of the day wisely took a hands-off, laissez-faire attitude toward the economy and let it straighten itself out.

Herbert Hoover took a different approach. Perhaps fearing the political liability of being in office at the start of the Depression, Hoover took a more active role in putting American business back on its feet. Hoover undertook a campaign of increased government spending to stimulate the economy. By the standards of the time, the program was one of immense proportions. It was only after the even greater spending plans of succeeding presidents that Hoover acquired his reputation as a fiscal conservative. Hoover's meddling, of course, brought predictable results: the economy grew worse. The worse things got, the more Hoover intervened, and the economy continued to struggle.

The 1932 presidential campaign pitted Hoover, the fiscal liberal, against Franklin D. Roosevelt, the conservative. The Democratic economic platform read:

> We advocate:
>
> 1. An immediate and drastic reduction of governmental expenditures by abolishing useless commissions and offices, consolidating departments and bureaus and eliminating extravagance, to accomplish a saving of not less than 25 percent in the cost of federal government.
>
> 2. Maintenance of the national credit by a federal budget annually balanced.
>
> 3. A sound currency to be maintained at all hazards.[4]

The American people were not economic illiterates. They understood, as their forefathers did, the value of limited government. Roosevelt lambasted Hoover for heading the greatest peace-time spending administration in the country's history.

Once in office Roosevelt took up the task of ending the Depression. In his inaugural address, the president stated that he wished to keep a proper balance between the executive and legislative branches of the government. He added that should Congress be lax in dealing with the Depression, he would ask Congress for more power.

The American nation breathed a sigh of relief as finally they had in office a man dedicated to fiscal sanity and limited government. Then Roosevelt burned the party's platform and fanned the flame with his copy of Keynes's *General Theory*. Depressions happened because business was slow. Business was slow because people were not buying things. The solution was to encourage consumer spending through taxation, redistribution, and inflation. Taxation, redistribution, and inflation became Roosevelt's platform. An act of Congress allowed Roosevelt to follow through on his platform. The Congress declared, "All acts of the President and the Secretary of the Treasury since March 4th, 1933, are hereby confirmed and approved."[5] Roosevelt went to work on his new platform armed with a Congressional rubber stamp.

Roosevelt's national bank holiday took place for the purpose of finding which banks were stable and which unstable. It also enabled the president to find out who owned gold, and how much. The president decreed that all persons and corporations must hand over all gold holdings, or face fines and imprisonment. The American people assumed that this action was necessary for the nation's credit and that, once the crisis was over, they would redeem their paper dollars for gold. Nothing was said about devaluing the dollar or going off the gold standard.

Attached to the Emergency Farm Relief Act was the Inflation Amendment. This amendment enabled the president to use $3 billion at his own discretion and gave him the power to devalue the dollar by one-half. The government became an ever larger operation. Spending plans and redistribution programs of all kinds cropped up. Occasionally the Supreme Court reminded Roosevelt of his constitutional obligations, but his plan rolled along virtually unhindered.

Roosevelt quietly repudiated the gold standard. New laws enabled the government to pay its debts in any kind of money it felt suitable, and all debts, including private ones, could be paid for in paper money.

The words *legal tender* had long been seen on American paper money. In old Congressional records, these two words were explained: "Debts *may* be paid in this currency." Roosevelt's repudiation of the gold standard included one slight alteration of this definition. *Legal tender* now meant "Debts *must* be paid in this currency." Trade using gold was forbidden. America effectively had a money based on paper. Roosevelt himself declared each day the exchange rate of paper dollars to gold. Rumors spread that this decision was often made with the rolling of dice. Whatever the case, the price of gold inched up slowly as Roosevelt tried to put America to work and kept the printing presses working day and night. The Depression continued as Roosevelt surpassed his predecessor in interference and government spending. The American people stood in bread lines, forgetting the promises their president had made, and elected him to be their leader once more. Roosevelt offered more interference, more tampering, and an end to the Depression. The gold standard became a story for history books; inflation was the green wave of the future.

With the new onslaught of welfare and work programs, Hoover was viewed in a different light. He was the fiscal conservative, the tight-money president, and he was hated for it, just as he was once hated for being a fiscal liberal. No sirens rang, no alarms sounded, no Paul Revere rode through the countryside warning the people that the red ink was coming, red ink all over federal budgets from Roosevelt's time to the present. The problem is not that once off the gold standard the government *might* inflate the money supply; the problem is that they have and will probably continue to do so.

Governments, when given the freedom, almost always counterfeit. There are only two ways to pay for government, taxation and inflation. Taxation shows up in your paycheck every week. You know what the government is withholding from you, but you don't know how much paper money they are printing.

The inflated dollar is a weakened dollar. The dollar buys less and less. Inflation is not increased prices, but devalued dollars. Inflated dollars are really deflated dollars, deflated of their value and purchasing power.

During the regime of President Carter, the nightly news kept us posted on the price of gold and on the exchange rates of dollars to various foreign currencies which enjoyed a higher degree of stability than our own. The nation began to worry as the dollar fell steadily, day after day, in relation to gold and to foreign currencies. The inflation rate neared 20 percent. Gold climbed over the eight-hundred-dollars-an-ounce mark. Less than thirty years ago, gold could be bought for one-twentieth of that. Inflation was hitting the country hard, and the news reported the casualties daily to a worried America.

Inflation has the same effect on international trade as it does on lenders. Wary of receiving devalued dollars, foreign businesses shy away from trade with America. Unstable currencies frighten everyone away. Inflated dollars are like hot potatoes—no one wants to be caught holding them.

International trade between two countries who are off the gold standard is dangerous business. No one knows just exactly how much another's system has been inflated. That is why exchange rates fluctuate so much so quickly. In a gold-based world money system, exchange rates are figured in terms of gold, and never change. A stable atmosphere is more open to international trade and thus to international mutual profit. Inflation makes international trade hazardous, taking away greater opportunities for profit. Inflation discourages international consumer spending, a Keynesian horror, a mercantilist delight. The devalued dollar hurts all businesses, especially those involved in international trade. The volume of international trade in nations with highly devalued currency is a pittance when measured against the volume of trade in countries with relatively stable currencies.

When a country goes through a period of devaluation, all its currency held in foreign countries tends to return to the home country. Just as Americans do not want their money sitting in banks losing its value, foreigners do not want to hold American money while its value shrinks. As a result, American dollars are returned to America quickly, bringing still more inflation and devaluation as the money supply grows. American dollars pour back into the country to stay.

Inflation hurts international trade much the same way that it hurts domestic trade. A feeling of distrust toward the currency encourages foreign companies to take their business elsewhere. That loss of trade translates to a loss of profit, the first point in our list of non-negotiables for material prosperity. As inflation encourages the return of American dollars from other countries, devaluation and distrust increase. Foreigners aren't forced to spend or save American dollars; they can simply trade for their native currency and watch the value of the once strong American dollar fall.

Inflation is not a cold technical problem. It is not an academic phenomenon. I do not rest my case against inflation solely on natural economic laws or on our God-given power of reason. I am not concerned solely over the lost value of my bank account or over the departure from the ways of the father of economics, Adam Smith. I do not write as an anachronistic gold-bug prophet. I am not an old Republican looking under every rock to find every bit of filth I can place on Franklin Delano Roosevelt. Inflation is a Christian concern, not in some vague sense of stewardship or drive to build the kingdom of God. Inflation is a problem that God speaks directly to. Not merely an unwise and painful mistake, inflation is a sin, a violation of the law of God.

Inflation is a violation of God's general law. Just as a man who attempts to break God's law of gravity by stepping off the top of a skyscraper will fall to his death, so also will a nation pay dearly for violating God's economic laws. Our economic problems today are not based on some natural boom and bust cycle, but they have their root in lawlessness, the lawlessness of an ever tampering, ever hampering, ever inflating, overgrowing government and the voting public. Economic predictions are easy: as long as the government interferes in the marketplace, one can expect economic problems. When the government backs away from the market, only then will we experience economic growth and well-being.

Inflation is not merely a violation of God's general law; it bears the judgment of God in Scripture. Just as false weights and measures are forbidden in the marketplace, so also are they forbidden to the government. The use of false weights and measures in the Old Testament was an act of devaluation, an act of stealing value from another. So also is inflation an act of devaluation. The dollar today is not the dollar of ten years ago. Neither is a quarter what it used to be. Look at the side of any quarter. This Oreo design is not for decoration; it is the intrusion of cheap metals into our coins. The government that can produce a quarter for five cents turns quite a profit. The cheaper the metals are, the more profit the government makes. The American government is weighing our money with smaller and smaller stones day by day.

The same judgment which stood on the dishonest trader of the Old Testament stands on our government today. *Dross* is the Old Testament word describing the impurities added to coins. Just as the impurities of our hearts cannot escape the eye of God, so also the impurities of coins do not escape his eye and judgment. In the first chapter of the book of Isaiah, God declares his judgment upon his chosen race. Isaiah lists many of their sins. One of them is the devaluation of coinage. "How is the faithful city become an harlot! it was full of judgment; righteousness lodged in it; but now murderers. Thy silver is become dross, thy wine mixed with water: Thy princes are rebellious, and companions of thieves: every one loveth gifts, and followeth after rewards: they judge not the fatherless, neither doth the cause of the widow come unto them" (Isa. 1:21–23). Isaiah is not telling Israel that their silver has miraculously changed to worthless dross. He is bringing an indictment from the mouth of God against this inflation. Inflation is a transgression against a righteous God.[6]

Ex-president Jimmy Carter recently graced the cover of a widely read national evangelical magazine under the title "Keeping Faith," the title of his recent book. Carter, in both the book and the magazine, tells of his spiritual struggles in office and the strength of

Christ which he relied on. We wonder if Mr. Carter ever read Isaiah 1. The Carter administration printed more paper dollars than any one before its time. Why? A judgment of charity demands that this policy was practiced in ignorance. Yet it remains an immoral policy.

There has been little moral outrage about the systematic debasing of currency in the United States. Coalitions form to fight racism, sexism, violence on television, pornography, pollution, extinction, nuclear wars, any wars, creedism, fascism, and communism. The list is endless, but where is the People's Anti-Inflation Network? Why are the prudent savers in our country not marching on Washington demanding an end to the devaluation of our money? Perhaps we Christians think we should not be concerned about base, materialistic subjects such as money. Perhaps we should be more concerned with more spiritual matters. But sin is a spiritual matter, and inflation is sin. Isaiah, who spoke the words of God, was concerned about inflation.

Jimmy Carter, our born-again former president and greatest inflator in American history, once said of inflation that it is "the cruelest tax of all." Inflation is the only form of taxation in America today that is not graduated. The minimum wage laborer loses the value of his money at the same rate as a million-dollar-a-year star athlete. Inflation knows no classes, no tax brackets; it robs indiscriminately. Yet the hardest hit are the poor and the elderly with fixed incomes. Here is where the cruelty is most painfully felt.

It is often hypothesized that the people will not stand for taxation above 25 percent. Our American Revolution was fought over a tax rate that we can only dream of today. Governments have a habit of promising more and more benefits with each election. We trade votes for the promise of money from the government. Pork-barrel politicians are not run out of Washington on a rail for their dishonesty and corruption; they are hailed by their constituents, elected, and re-elected until someone else promises more benefits. The politician promising to tax is despised. The one who promises to spend is revered.

Everyone hates taxation; everyone loves to receive government money. Before we withdrew from the gold standard, the politician was in a bind. This bind kept the cost and size of government down and American prosperity up. Once the government was freed from the gold standard, it was freed from this bind. Taxation is the money that the government takes from individuals. This is what politicians are forced to keep down. Inflation, however, allows the politician to promise government financial support to every cause and its corollary. Inflation is a blank check, covered and insured only by the printing press.

But inflation, the printing of fiat money, diminishes purchasing power. Through inflation, the government takes away the value of the money that remains in your hands after taxation. The government "taxes" your purchasing power by flooding the marketplace with crisp new counterfeit bills. This too is taxation, the kind that need not be mentioned in campaign speeches. This taxation doesn't show up under "withheld"; it shows up in higher prices around the country where businessmen rather than politicians take the blame. Our dollars do not actually and visibly shrink; their purchasing power shrinks. Apparently few people make the connection between higher grocery bills and deficit spending in Washington. The connection is indirect but real. This cruel tax is silent but devastating.

This cruel tax is covert, carried on behind the closed doors of government. No one announces that the government will take a given percentage of your purchasing power in the next fiscal year. No one announces just how much the government's fiscal policies will cost your savings account. The cruelest tax of all has continued since the days of F.D.R. The American people remain in an economic slumber. Our money is losing its value day by day. We hear more and more rhetoric from our presidents, but we continue to see red ink on the budget year after year. The dollar inflates as its purchasing power declines. Nixon tried price controls; Carter tried "guidelines." But the budgets still do not balance, and the presses keep printing. Where is Isaiah? The unemployment lines, the shutdown factories, and higher bills are only the beginning of the inevitable economic collapse brought on by inflation.

The Statue of Liberty stands in New York Harbor welcoming all who yearn to be free. The statue is a symbol of hope, a symbol of the American dream. Thousands come to our shores, hoping that in this, the freest country in the world, they can be prosperous.

People of all nations have fled poverty, war, famine, discrimination, and totalitarian regimes to live in America and be free.

The story is often repeated. A young man from Eastern Europe books passage across the Atlantic on a freighter. Upon arrival in New York, he finds hard, but steady, work. He lives modestly, saving nearly all his wages to pay the way for his family to join him. The family reunites, but the modest living and prudent saving continue. The children are encouraged to work hard in school. One may earn a university scholarship, another may use the accumulated savings to start a small business. After graduation the children are able to find good jobs, get married, and move into houses of their own. In two generations, a family has moved from a sod house in Eastern Europe to a heated house with indoor plumbing and a car in the garage.

But the story is changing, although some parts remain. People around the world still live a peasant's life of poverty. Many still believe in the value of hard work and education. The dream of owning a house still lives in the hearts of many. What is different today? The power of saving is gone. The hope of prudent living and saving to escape conditions of poverty is no longer viable. If this same immigrant were to cross the ocean today, find work, and save, his chances of success would be less. Inflation takes from his bank account. The more this man saves, the more he loses. And so the poor remain poor. Inflation, the great stimulator of consumer demand, the economic pick-me-up of Keynes, leaves the poor in the slums with no means of escape. The dream is shattered by politicians' efforts to find a means of spending without taxing. The huddled masses come to America to huddle in masses here. The inscription on the Statue of Liberty is an anachronism in the modern world of budget deficits. The government has taken away the ticket out of the slum, saving. Then it tries to cure resulting ills with endless social programs based on more spending, higher deficits, and more inflation.

Earlier in the chapter I discussed the havoc which inflation plays with capital investment. Shrinking savings accounts and high inflationary risk drive up interest rates, making investment in new tools of production difficult and ofttimes impossible. Perhaps I was unable to raise sympathy for the corporate executives who are unable to expand and increase their profit due to inflationary pressures against investment. Not only does this lack of investment hit the executive in the wallet, it is another powerful force in the continuance of poverty. While bankers and businessmen in tailored suits sit in leather chairs talking over the investment difficulties that inflation presents, the new immigrant sits in his dimly-lit, one-room apartment—unemployed. He is unemployed because we live in a stagnant economy, stagnant from lack of investment. That lack of investment exists because of the many paper fiat dollars in our system.

The futility of saving hits both the poor man and the rich man. However, the poor man pays for both his own and the rich man's inability to save. The rich man cannot save; hence he cannot invest. Since he cannot invest, his business cannot grow and he cannot hire more workers. And that is why the poor man sits in his slum, unemployed.

Going back to our non-negotiables for material prosperity, we can see where inflation has torpedoed the program. In an inflated economy, saving is foolish. But we cannot enjoy material well-being without savings. If the prosperity cycle is broken, people of all economic levels are affected, from the multimillionaire to the low-skilled laborer. Those least able to deal with the problem are the poor. The work ethic does not say, "Work hard and you'll go places," but rather, "Work hard, *save*, and you'll go places." If one doesn't save, he can go nowhere. If one does save, and his money is losing its value to inflation, he can get nowhere. It is the poor who bear the brunt of the evil of inflation. Certainly all struggle against it, but the poor have no back-up resources. If they cannot find work, they cannot provide for themselves and their families.

Why then, if inflation creates this multitude of problems, do we have inflation? Who is benefiting from it? Those who reap the greatest rewards are the politicians who live off the ignorance of the populace. They are able to promise endless programs, taking full credit, and putting the blame of inflation on someone else. They are elected on promises of more money for the home state and lower taxes, and they blame the deficit on anything from defense spending to the length of women's skirts. The charade continues year after year. Also benefiting from inflation are those receiving the money first. Let us return to my nightmare of counterfeiting to illustrate.

Having a deficit in my budget, I create fiat money with my basement printing press. This increase in the money supply devalues my money as well as everyone else's. The result is inevitably an increase in prices. Prices do not rise immediately, however. When I first spend my counterfeit dollars, there is no rise in prices because no one is yet aware of this inflation. The recipient of my money will likewise probably be able to spend the money without losing out to higher prices. Eventually the word gets out that bogus money is in circulation and then prices begin to rise.

Those who benefit the most from inflation are those on the government payroll—defense contractors, public employees, federal relief recipients, social security recipients, all the countless millions who at one time or another receive a check from the federal government—since they receive the inflated money first, before its value has had a chance to go down. This fiat money is passed on until it reaches the lowest echelons, the poor, those who are least aware of the complexities of economics. They are the ones who get caught holding the funny money, and they pay for it dearly.

Inflation benefits the wheeling-dealing politicians of our day, giving them the power to buy votes, literally. Every federal program, be it low cost housing, sewage systems, defense factories, or a power plant such as the Tennessee Valley Authority, comes via the courtesy of inflation. Every raised price, every increase in the interest rate, every devaluation of your savings comes to us ultimately from the Bureau of Engraving and Printing.

Inflation helps the government, and it helps those whom the government professes to help. Those who receive money from the government get a big jump in the race against inflation. They can spend the new money before the word is out. The vote buyers and the vote sellers benefit from inflation.

Inflation is not higher prices. This must be so ingrained into our thinking that every time a newscaster reads an inflation rate that is actually the rate of price increases, our skin should crawl. The truth that our government would like to keep hidden is that *inflation is an increase in the money supply.* The government does not control prices (usually), but it does control the money supply.

Inflation is an increase in the money supply. The responsibility for inflation rests solely on the heads of government, the federal government. Inflation is not the scheme of a butcher hoping for a second car; it is the scheme of countless government officials hoping for a second term.

Inflation is an exercise in the production of fiat money. Webster's defines fiat money as paper currency made legal tender by law or fiat, although not backed by gold or silver and not necessarily redeemable in coin. This is an apt description of our American dollar. Our money is fiat money backed by order of the government and nothing else. The word *fiat* indicates the problems of fiat money. The government's declaration that green paper is money is akin to my declaring my dog a cat. Surely I have the authority to do this, inasmuch as the dog belongs to me; but I do not have the power. Neither does the government have the power to make paper have real value.

The government stands guilty of breaking its own laws. It has set itself above the law in the act of counterfeiting. The Federal Reserve, the president and the legislature all take part in this. Perhaps the law against counterfeiting exists only to protect the government, to insure a monopoly in printing money. The government will allow no one to share in the glory of counterfeiting.

The government not only prevents competition in the paper money business, but also forbids any other form of money (for example, real money like gold or silver). Legal tender laws now prevent the use of anything but devalued paper and devalued coins issued by the government in any trade transactions. All trade in America takes place with the medium of exchange that the government dictates, government fiat money and nothing else. The government protects itself on all sides by denying any other medium of exchange.

If we are to stop the unethical and economically destructive use of inflation as a tool of government interventionism, it is necessary to do more than turn off the money machine. As long as the government has the money machine and the legal power to use it, the odds are that the "on" switch will be pressed again. This is especially likely if the federal deficit continues to swell and budgets continue unbalanced. The machine must either be destroyed or limited to printing money that has hard value behind it. No law requires that our paper currency be backed by hard money of some sort. As long as this situation exists, the government has the legal right (but not the moral right) to counterfeit.

SEVEN
BIBLICAL CONCERN
FOR THE POOR

The phrase *the poor* functions as more than a working definition for a group of people lacking material goods. Not only is *the poor* a descriptive term; it is an emotive term, one that provokes feelings ranging from compassion to fury. The mere mention of the poor can provoke political zeal; it can be a rallying cry for revolution. On the lips of a demagogue it becomes a cry for political action. On the lips of an elitist it becomes a contemptuous epithet. So much unspoken and undefined excess baggage accompanies the phrase that it begs for more sober qualification.

We must ask questions such as, Who are the poor? Why are they poor? What does it mean to be poor? We need clear definition and at least a basic understanding of the root causes of poverty if we are to cut through the emotive and penetrate to the substantive.

Poor is a relative term. It assumes some standard of wealth. Poverty levels are adjusted from culture to culture, from generation to generation, even from year to year. The current poverty level of income would have placed a family in the middle class in 1950 and in the upper middle class in 1900. As the purchasing power of the dollar fluctuates, so does the poverty level. If we define poverty as a lack of material goods, again we face a problem of relativity. If a person living in the United States in the modern era lived his days without benefit of indoor plumbing or electricity, he might easily be called poor. Yet little more than a century ago, even the upper classes used outhouses and candles.

In our efforts to clarify the meaning of poverty, we must at some point go beyond such cultural relativities and define the essentials that the poor lack entirely or have in inadequate amounts. We may include only such necessities as food, clothing, shelter, and health care, or we may go beyond these to more relative areas such as education, transportation, tools of production, and other material benefits in addition to the bare essentials of subsistence.

Are we, when we use the catch word *poor*, speaking of people who are starving to death for lack of food or freezing to death for lack of clothing and shelter; or are we speaking of people who lack educational opportunity, sophisticated tools, or modern means of transportation? A native islander may be well fed and adequately clothed and housed, yet still be using a mule instead of a tractor. He may have the bare necessities of life, indeed may have the "riches" of a tribal chieftain, yet still be poor in terms of worldwide standards of living.

We see then that poverty is not a static absolute. It is better defined in terms of a continuum with two poles ranging from extreme poverty where even the bare necessities of life are lacking, through the midpoint of reasonable comfort, to the opposite pole of opulent luxury.

	poverty	**wealth**	
subsistence			**luxury**

As long as one person exists who lacks something that another enjoys, we can speak of a relative continuum. Unless all wealth were somehow distributed absolutely equally, there would be some meaning to the relative terms *rich* and *poor*.

Jesus' statement, "Ye have the poor always with you" (Mt. 26:11), does not mean "You can't do anything about poverty"; nor does it indicate that Jesus was unconcerned about the plight of the poor. His was not a statement of passive resignation to an unalterable human dilemma. Jesus' life was a portrait of energetic ministry to the poor. His ethic is one of compassionate concern for the poor. That the poor are always with us is not a license for indifference but a call to long-term ministry to them.

I once spoke to a minister who had devoted thirty years of daily ministry to the urban poor of Cleveland, Ohio. I asked how he endured the daily frustrations of his ministry over three decades. He replied, "I take comfort in Jesus' words, 'The poor you always have with you.' Many of my young assistants have grown disillusioned and bitter after two or three years. Their idealism was shattered when their seminary dreams of eliminating poverty were not quickly realized. I understand that my job is not to eliminate poverty but to bring the compassion of Christ to bear on it every day."

To be sure, the minister was doing more than giving alms. He was attacking the root causes of poverty in his neighborhood. He was working relentlessly *toward* the elimination of poverty, knowing full well that however much progress he achieved he would not be able to eliminate poverty altogether.

To deal effectively and properly with poverty, we must first distinguish different kinds of poverty. Here the Bible is not silent.

In the Old Testament, just treatment in the law courts is of primary importance to concern for the poor. Yehezkel Kaufmann in his important work, *The Religion of Israel*, maintains:

> Every Israelite is enjoined from showing partiality, taking bribes, and perverting justice (Exod. 23:3, 7ff.; Lev. 19:15, 35, etc.). The duty of dealing rightly with the poor and the helpless is emphasized (Exod. 23:6; Deut. 24:17; 27:19); God himself is the model in biblical justice. Israelite law—as distinct from other Near Eastern law—recognizes no class privileges.[7]

In Israel, Justice was to keep her blindfold on. She was not allowed to peek. The guiding principle was *no partiality* before the bar of justice. Not only was it forbidden to grant special favors to the rich and powerful, but it was also forbidden to give the poor special treatment. "Do not show favoritism to a poor man in his lawsuit" (Exod. 23:3, NIV). The law is succinctly stated in Leviticus 19:15: "Thou shalt not respect the person of the poor, nor honour the person of the mighty: but in righteousness shalt thou judge thy neighbour." The curse of God falls upon those who take advantage of the weak or helpless in the courtroom (Deut. 27:19).

Karl Marx complained that laws in capitalistic societies tend to reflect the vested interests of the ruling classes. The rich and powerful will, according to Marx, ultimately influence legislation that will give them an edge in economic competition. Yet de Tocqueville warned that the edge can be gained by either side. The powerful will influence legislation, but the powerful are not always the rich. The political power of large voting blocs can offset the individual power of a single wealthy individual. In a society where the majority rules, the majority can exercise a tyranny over the minority. De Tocqueville's warning that the democratic experiment of the United States may be destroyed "when the people discover that they can vote themselves largesse" is already a fulfilled prophecy. The graduated income tax, for example, is a glaring indication that partiality is shown to the poor. The wealthy who are in the higher income brackets represent a powerless minority who are obvious victims of economic injustice.

Israel had no provision for lobby groups or special-interest groups. The guiding principle was *rule by law*, not *rule by men*. Just laws of impartiality were to be sacrosanct. They were not to be changed or repealed, whether by the whims of malevolent tyrants or by the self-serving interests of a voting majority. There are essentially four different causes of poverty mentioned in the Bible, each kind demanding a different reaction from the Christian. We must understand these distinctions if we wish to ameliorate the problem. These four different causes of poverty are *slothfulness*, *calamity*, *exploitation*, and *personal sacrifice*. To lump these four groups together, seeking a common solution, is as foolish as trying to cure cancer, heart disease, the common cold, and insomnia with one pill.

The Bible is clear in speaking out against those who are poor because they are lazy. Laziness is a real and serious human problem. It involves a refusal to carry out God's creation mandate to work. Karl Barth listed sloth as one of the primary and foundational sins of man, along with pride and dishonesty. According to Barth, this triad of vices constitutes the root causes of all other sins.[8]

God comes down hard on the slothful, saying, "Go to the ant, thou sluggard; consider her ways, and be wise" (Prov. 6:6). It is a pitiful and sinful man who must look to insects for instruction. God values and commands hard work from his people, a command both the wealthy and the poor dare not overlook. Paul speaks of the slothful poor when he says, "If any would not work, neither should he eat" (2 Thess. 3:10). Here compassion is limited by the demand for work. Slothfulness is not to be indulged by the Christian community.

It is difficult to be lazy and not be poor; but it is possible to be poor and not be lazy. Understanding this principle is crucial if we are to withstand the temptation of reducing all poverty to the single cause of slothfulness. It would be convenient to assume that the only cause for poverty is slothfulness. If this were so, we could be justified in closing our ears to the poor, leaving them to their just deserts. Sloth is one cause of poverty, but by no means the only cause.

Those suffering under other forms of poverty need a different reaction from the Christian community, one of compassion, understanding, and aid. The lazy have only themselves to blame for their poverty and will be required to answer for it before our holy God. We, however, will be held accountable before God for how we react to those suffering poverty for other reasons.

The second group is poor as a result of calamity. The Scriptures recognize that many are made poor by disease or disasters. The man born blind, the person left crippled by an accident, the farmer whose crops have been destroyed by flood or drought—all have just cause for their impoverished state.

Let us use Job as our example. Job was a hard-working, God-fearing, wealthy man. Tragedy struck again and again, leaving Job a broken man. His friends ran to his side, not to show compassion or to help, but to accuse Job of deplorable sins. But the Lord allows rain to fall on the fields of the good and the bad, and he likewise allows floods to cover the fields of the wicked and the righteous (see Mt. 5:45). We cannot determine the secret counsel of God in these events, but are called to respond to God's revealed commands to assist the victims of disaster. To these victims, we are to show compassion and genuine charity. It is the responsibility of God's people to see to it that the suffering of these people is ameliorated. They are to be a priority concern of the church; they are the hungry who are to be fed, the naked who are to be clothed (see Mt. 25:31–46). People struck by calamities are to be cared for.

The third group is poor as a result of exploitation. These are the poor who suffer indignities when they live in societies where the social, political, and judicial institutions favor the rich and powerful and leave the poor without advocacy. One such society was Israel in the eighth century B.C., when "the poor were sold for a pair of shoes." God came down hard on that society through his prophets. This kind of oppression provokes God; he hears the moans of his people. Such injustice should likewise move the church to legitimate social action.

Finally some are poor as the result of personal sacrifice. In the New Testament, these are referred to as the poor for righteousness' sake.[9] This group is made up of people who are voluntarily poor. Their poverty is a result of conscious decisions to choose life-styles or vocations with little or no financial remuneration. This class of poor are promised special blessings from God. They are poor because their priorities do not mesh with the value standards of the culture in which they live. These include Martin Luther, passing up a promising and lucrative career to wear a monk's habit; they include the modern businessman who passes up the windfall deal because he has scruples about hidden unethical elements.

The distinctions between kinds of poverty are essential. We must not succumb to the tendency to generalize about poverty; we may not lump the poor together in one package. At the same time, we must avoid the equally dangerous temptation of grouping together the rich. It would be unjust and slanderous to maintain that all rich people are corrupt, as if all riches were achieved through evil means or through exploiting the poor. Not all rich people are ruthless people feeding off the poor. To find examples of wealthy men who were righteous, we need go no further than Scripture, which gives us Abraham, Job, David, and Joseph of Arimathea.

We must recognize that God cares deeply about human poverty and the suffering that is so often closely associated with it. Our duty as Christians is to be no less concerned than God himself. As long as the poor are with us, we are called to minister to them, not only through charity, but by seeking and working for the reformation of social and political structures which enslave, oppress, and exploit them.

The Bible sets down laws on how to deal with the poor. The poor-laws of the Bible give us a way of dealing with poverty that is far greater than any elaborate Great Society scheme. The Bible calls us to personal, concrete action on behalf of the poor.

Those singled out by Scripture who demand our attention are widows and orphans. Exodus 22:22–24 reads: "Ye shall not afflict any widow, or fatherless child. If thou afflict them in any wise, and they cry at all unto me, I will surely hear their cry; and my wrath shall wax hot, and I will kill you with the sword; and your wives shall be widows, and your children fatherless." Dealing with these oppressed people is a core obligation of our religion. James 1:27 reads, "Pure religion and undefiled before God and the Father is this, To visit the fatherless and widows in their affliction, and to keep himself unspotted from the world." Paul told Timothy to "honor widows" (1 Tim. 5:3). The Greek word translated "honor" is often used in Scripture to indicate payment, and it is obviously used in that manner here. Paul does, however, set limits on giving to widows. Regular support must be given only to those who are truly widows, who are without family, too old to remarry, and thus unable to receive support from relatives. The restrictions run still deeper. Only the widow who is engaged in charitable service is eligible to receive the church's support. She must be "well known for her good deeds, such as bringing up children, showing hospitality, washing the feet of the saints, helping those in trouble and devoting herself to all kinds of good deeds" (1 Tim. 5:10, NIV). Biblical charity does not subsidize the slothful.

The chain of responsibility in dealing with poverty is simple. The point man is the family, the first in line to care for the poor. The second scout is the church, taking over the responsibility if there is not family. The Bible calls for responsible action by families and individuals.

Auberon Herbert said more than a century ago:

> So long as great government departments . . . supply our wants, so long shall we remain in our present condition, the difficulties of life unconquered, and ourselves unfitted to conquer them. No amount of state education will make a really intelligent nation; no amount of Poor Laws will place a nation above want; no amount of Factory Acts will make us better parents. These great wants which we are now vainly trying to deal with by acts of Parliament, by prohibitions and penalties, are in truth the great occasions of progress, if only we surmount them by developing in ourselves more active desires, by putting forth greater efforts, by calling new moral forces into existence, and by perfecting our national ability for acting together in voluntary associations. To have our wants supplied from without by a huge state machinery, to be regulated and inspected by great armies of officials, who are themselves slaves to the system which they administer, will in the long run teach us nothing, will profit us nothing.

Christian giving is not impersonal, computerized distribution of wealth. Christian giving is personal care, the kind of care which in love encourages the recipients to get back on their feet again soon. Our goal as Christians should not be to make sure that the poor are fed, but rather to insure that the poor are fed through biblical means. Paul writes to Timothy, "If any provide not for his own, and specially for those of his own house, he hath denied the faith, and is worse than an infidel" (1 Tim. 5:8). The words of Paul, God's apostle, do not read, "If anyone does not see to it that his own are provided for." A man must provide for his family, for his parents, for his relatives who need him. He is not to pass the responsibility on to the government, which surely is better equipped in that it holds the power of taxation. It is the man's job, and he is called "worse than an infidel" if he does not do it. These are strong words, words we dare not overlook. God wants to build responsible relationships within families.

The family holds first responsibility in caring for the poor. There are, however, poor without family, and poor without responsible family. In such cases, the church bears the responsibility for their care. It must be remembered that the church is not merely the organized institution of the worshiping assembly; the church is the people of God.

Old Testament Israel had a system of not one tithe, but three. The first tithe went to the Levites. The Levites were not just official priests. They were also teachers, musicians, judges, and physicians. Most of the tithe, in fact, went to people who were not priests. This illustrates a principle we should not overlook: our tithe today need not all go directly to the church; other institutions need our financial support also. Our tithe may go to some Christian educational organization; it may support a Christian hospital or Christian missions. Building the kingdom of God, like building a successful business, requires investment capital; it requires our tithes.

The second tithe, another 10 percent tax on increase, was used for a yearly festival gathering. One tenth of a family's income was to be spent having a party. Deuteronomy 14:26 reads, "And thou shalt bestow that money for whatsoever thy soul lusteth after, for oxen, or for sheep, or for wine, or for strong drink, or for whatsoever thy soul desireth: and thou shalt eat there before the LORD thy God, and thou shalt rejoice, thou, and thine household." This is a far cry from any Manichaean ideal of abstinence from physical pleasures. God calls us to rejoice in the abundance that comes from his blessing. Other cultures in the days of ancient Israel suffered famine and starvation, but Israel was still called to celebrate its bounty. God commanded that one tenth of Israel's income go toward this celebration of thanksgiving to God, the giver of material prosperity.

The third tithe was not annual, but was offered in the third and sixth years of every seven-year cycle. This tithe, known as the poor tithe, was used to feed the Levites, strangers, widows, and orphans who lived in the community. This tithe, though used only two years out of every seven, was not a substitute for the first of second tithe. It was a separate tithe and as binding as the first two (Deut. 14:20–29).

It is important to note that the Levites were included in this tithe. They were not recipients due to their state of poverty. On the contrary, Levites were generally the wealthiest group in Israelite society. They received benefits from all three tithes as a visual sign of the importance of God's law in society and of the necessity to further his Word in every area. The Old Testament model knows nothing of the modern "ideal" of keeping the clergy and other administrators of God's Word poor and humble.

The poor tithe was administered locally and personally. This is significant in light of our present-day problems of red tape and bureaucracy in dealing with the poor. The individual families in Israel, those paying the poor tithe, were required to have personal contact with the poor in their communities. This contact kept the well-to-do Israelites aware of the condition of the poor, and it ensured that money was given to the truly needy. Poverty, for most Americans, is as distant as a big-city ghetto or the highlands of the Kentucky Appalachians. We soothe our consciences by writing checks, but we stay clear of meeting poverty face to face. Old Testament Israel had to face the poor; they had to see the conditions and become personally involved in the care of the poor.

The poor tithe had safeguards against supporting irresponsibility. Tithers kept their money from the lazy; they diverted it from the slothful. The poor man could not count on a continuous supply of free food. The poor tithe was collected only two years in seven. God showed mercy on the poor by commanding charity to them and by keeping the wealthy aware of their plight. But the poor did not have a running claim on the beneficence of the rich. The principle that Paul later stated also applied in Old Testament Israel: if a man wouldn't work, he couldn't eat. The wealthy were responsible to contribute the poor tithe. The poor were responsible to find gainful employment, to pull themselves out of poverty and become productive citizens of God's kingdom. The poor laws were not designed to subsidize poverty.

Murray Rothbard, in his voluminous work *Man, Economy and State*, writes:

> State poor relief is clearly a subsidization of poverty, for men are now automatically entitled to money from the state because of their poverty. Hence, the marginal disutility of income foregone from leisure diminishes, and idleness and poverty tend to increase further, which in turn increases the amount of subsidy that must be extracted from the taxpayers. Thus, a system of legally subsidized poverty tends to call forth more of the very poverty that is supposedly being alleviated. A man will not work if he is assured of minimal comforts not working. The reason to work is simply not there as a man today can be paid by the government to not work.[10]

God's system avoids this problem by making it economically desirable to work one's way out of poverty. Rothbard writes on private charity: "Private charity to the poor, on the other hand, would not have the same vicious-circle effect, since the poor would not have a continuing compulsory claim on the rich. This is particularly true where private charity is given only to the 'deserving' poor." Under the biblical poor laws, the vicious circle is avoided. Poverty is neither subsidized nor ignored.[11]

Gleaning was the only regular charity which the poor of Israel received. Farmers were forbidden to harvest the corners of their fields. Fruit which remained on the trees after they had been beaten and shaken had to remain there for the poor to pick. Leviticus 19:9, 10 reads:

> When ye reap the harvest of your land, thou shalt not wholly reap the corners of thy field, neither shalt thou gather the gleanings of thy harvest. And thou shalt not glean thy vineyard, neither shalt thou gather every grape of thy vineyard; thou shalt leave them for the poor and stranger: I am the LORD your God.

Dueteronomy 24:19–22 further elaborates:

> When thou cuttest down thine harvest in thy field, and hast
> forgot a sheaf in the field, thou shalt not go again to fetch it:
> it shall be for the stranger, for the fatherless, and for the
> widow: that the LORD thy God may bless thee in all the work
> of thine hands. When thou beatest thine olive tree, thou shalt
> not go over the boughs again: it shall be for the stranger, for
> the fatherless, and for the widow. When thou gatherest the
> grapes of thy vineyard, thou shalt not glean it afterward: it
> shall be for the stranger, for the fatherless, and for the widow.
> And thou shalt remember that thou wast a bondman in the
> land of Egypt: therefore I command thee to do this thing.

Gleaning laws reflected God's compassion for the poor, but they
did not foster irresponsibility. Gleaning did not amount to corporate
ownership of land. Landowners had the right to specify which of
the deserving poor could glean on their land. The story of Ruth
illustrates this.

> Then said Boaz unto Ruth, Hearest thou not, my daughter?
> Go not to glean in another field, neither go from hence, but
> abide here fast by my maidens: Let thine eyes be on the field
> that they do reap, and go thou after them: have I not charged
> the young men that they shall not touch thee? And when thou
> art athirst, go unto the vessels, and drink of that which the
> young men have drawn.

Ruth did not simply claim her "right" to glean, but bowed to the
ground in appreciation of the generosity and compassion of Boaz.
The responsibility of feeding the poor rested on the shoulders of the
citizens of Israel, not upon the government. The poor had no legal
claim to the fruit of the farmer's labor, yet they were fed.

Another aspect of gleaning differs greatly from our present system. Gleaning was hard work. Running to one's mailbox to receive
a government check hardly takes the energy out of a person. Gleaning was harder work than harvesting. The corners of fields quite

often lay in heavy thicket. The fruits that remained were few and hard to find, and still harder to pick. Gleaning was strenuous work. The poor could be fed through gleaning, but it was to one's advantage to find gainful employment. The lazy poor were not fed. They were not invited to glean. This biblical plan of charity nurtured responsibility, not welfare fraud, not hereditary poverty, not generation after generation of families fed by a bureaucratic welfare system.

EIGHT
EQUALITY VS. EQUITY

All of us, at one time or another, have had our heartfelt convictions attacked. It can be a confusing and disheartening experience. A man tells me that Jesus never rose from the dead, and that his ethical teachings were naive. I cannot understand why this man doubts that God has power over death. I cannot understand why he doubts the Word of God on the subject of right and wrong. At the same time, he cannot understand how I can put my trust in someone he sees as a desert-walking religious fanatic.

Similar misunderstandings exist in economics. To the socialist, the capitalist is an overweight, cigar-smoking man whose only guide in moral issues is dollars and cents. The conservative economist prefers a world where the haves prosper and the have-nots suffer; he defends the industrial pillaging of the earth, sweatshops, child labor, and rugged individualistic competition. It is not a pretty picture, nor is it an accurate one. Vision becomes distorted when we enter the political arena. The conservative looks at a socialist through equally jaundiced eyes. Socialists are caricatured as hardened revolutionaries seeking to burn our sacred Constitution, to destroy our national wealth, to enslave all of us, to destroy our freedom in the name of economic equality. This is a distorted picture of what a socialist actually wants. It obscures the most powerful impetus for socialism, compassion for the world's poor.

It is difficult to criticize an opponent fairly or to exercise judgment in charity. It is easy to succumb to the temptation of using worst-case analysis for the other side while reserving the right of best-case analysis for ourselves. Asking a political or economic conservative to describe a liberal is like asking a Hatfield to describe a McCoy. The result is more often slander and exaggeration than accuracy.

In writing this book, my objective has not been to praise socialism but to bury it. I am convinced that political and economic policies that involve the forcible redistribution of wealth via government intervention are neither right nor safe. My conviction is that such policies are both unethical and ineffective. They are not unethical *because* they are ineffective (the canon of moral judgment is not the slippery norm of pragmatism) but because they are wrong in principle. They violate both natural law (*lex naturalis*) and supernatural law (*lex aeternitatis*).

None of this negates the fact that the *intentions* of many, if not most, of those espousing such policies are honorable. The prime motive of socialism is to help the poor. The motive is noble and godly. God wants the poor helped. It would seem that, on the surface at least, socialists are on God's side. Unfortunately, their programs and means tend to foster greater poverty even though their hearts remain loyal to eliminating poverty. The tragic fallacy that invades socialist thinking is that there is a necessary causal connection between the wealth of the wealthy and the poverty of the poor. Socialists assume that one man's wealth is based on another man's poverty. Therefore, to stop poverty, to help the poor man, we must have socialism.

If the motive of socialism is to help the poor, the prime goal of a socialist state is to bring about equal distribution of wealth. There is a sharp contrast between the luxury of Beverly Hills and the misery of nearby Watts. The contrast produces a sense of holy anger. It seems unjust, immoral, and unbiblical for some to live so well and for others to be so poor. Equality of wealth would mean an end to this imbalance and apparent injustice. The highest expression of social justice, according to socialist theory, is not equal treatment under the law, but equal participation in wealth.

A teacher illustrated this equation of equal justice and equal wealth in a discussion with her junior-high-school students. The vast majority of the students agreed that the wealth of our country should be divided equally. The teacher argued against this conclusion but failed to persuade the youngsters otherwise. Days later the teacher returned a test her students had taken earlier. Each student received a grade of 72.6 percent. One student, who had answered all of the questions correctly, questioned his grade. The teacher explained that another student had not done very well on the test so she gave him some of the better student's points. To ensure a "fair" distribution of grades, she explained, she had divided the points equally among the students. The students, of course, objected to this new system. Once they had protested loudly enough, she reminded them of their discussion a few days earlier.

There is a subtle distinction, but one of paramount importance, between *equality* and *equity*. Equality is likeness, evenness, and uniformity. Equity is justice, impartiality, and fairness. Socialism calls for equality; the Scriptures call us to equity. Psalm 98:9 reads, "With righteousness shall he judge the world, and the people with equity." The distinction between equality and equity is blurred whenever the righteous call to equity leads to an unholy call to material equality.

The Bible is clear in its position. Although nowhere in the Old Testament do we find a hint of any legislation designed to bring material equality, we do find repeated warnings against inequity. Amos spoke out against unjust judges who were easily bribed, who used one system of law for the rich and another for the poor. A poor man during the days of Israel's apostasy had no chance of a fair ruling from a judge. Equity was nowhere to be found, and God's wrath burned. First Samuel 2:7 says, "The LORD maketh poor, and maketh rich." The Lord did not build an egalitarian society based on the equal redistribution of wealth.

The word *equality* appears two times in the New Testament. In 2 Corinthians 8:13–15, Paul asks that the church at Corinth financially assist the needy Christians in Jerusalem: "For I mean not that other men be eased and ye burdened: but by an equality, that now at this time your abundance may be a supply for their want, that their abundance also may be a supply for your want: that there may be equality. As it is written, He that had gathered much had nothing over; and he that had gathered little had no lack."

Here Paul is not advocating the equal redistribution of wealth, but rather that the Corinthians voluntarily help out in a time of need in Jerusalem. Equality here is not used in an absolute leveling sense, but means that all should have enough to eat. Philip Hughes writes:

> As Hodge points out, what Paul is advocating here "is not agrarianism, nor community of goods," for in the New Testament all giving is voluntary and the fruit of love. Its object is the relief of want, not an artificial equalization of property. . . . Thus . . . the Scriptures avoid, on the one hand, the injustice and destructive evils of agrarian communism, by recognizing the right of property and making all almsgiving optional; and on the other, the heartless disregard of the poor by inculcating the universal brotherhood of believers, and the consequent duty of each to contribute of his abundance to relieve the necessities of the poor. [12]

Colossians 4:1 reads, "Masters, give unto your servants that which is just and equal." Paul is not calling for socialistic income redistribution here either, but rather is demanding that slave holders be responsible and insure the necessities of life for their slaves.

The principle here is fairness. The slave master is reminded that he too has a Master in heaven. This is a simple application of the golden rule, not a credo for egalitarianism. Lightfoot adds:

> It seems a mistake to suppose that ἰσότης here has anything to do with the treatment of slaves *as equals* (comp. Philem 16). When connected with ζίκαιον, the word naturally suggests an evenhanded, impartial treatment and is equivalent to the Latin *aequitas*. [13]

Paul is saying, then, that a wealthy slave owner and the slave himself are equal if they both have enough to eat.

Our Declaration of Independence holds as a self-evident truth that all men are created equal. The framers of the Declaration knew full well that in the colonies some men were more wealthy than others. They did not seek to change this. Their concern was for justice, not equality of wealth. All men, poor or wealthy, farmer or merchant, deserve equal justice under the law. No man is to receive preferential treatment in the courts.

Legal justice and economic equality are not the same thing. Though both involve a kind of equality, the equality has two different referents. Equality in a judicial sense is impartiality in judgment; equality of wealth is the even distribution of goods and services to all people.

Equality of material ownership may be a noble ideal in a world where sin is not present. It may be that if all people were equally industrious, equally productive, and equally prudent, and if all were equally in need, then justice might require equal distribution of wealth. But to enforce such an equality in a world where some are industrious while others are slothful, and some are productive while others are wasteful, is not to establish justice but to destroy it. In such a system, equity is swallowed up by equality.

Advocates of a transfer society in which the power of the state is used to force a redistribution of wealth constantly couch their platforms in two noble phrases, "social justice" and "the goal of economic equality." These twin concepts are noble in intention and might work in a sinless society. But to coerce economic equality in a sinful society is to perform social injustice. Here the redistributionist is guilty of calling evil good. His end is noble, but his means ignoble; his goal is altruistic, but his methods are tyrannical. The only way to have a transfer society is to violate justice. The cornerstone of most redistributionist policies is legalized theft: taking from the rich, by force, and giving to the poor. Now if the rich first gained their wealth by stealing from the poor, then the return of their property would merely be restitution. But redistributionism goes well beyond restitution to egalitarian transfers couched in euphemisms like "entitlements." The advocate of authentic social justice asks, "Why am I entitled to the fruit of another man's labor? What right do I have to my neighbor's property?"

God is no respecter of persons. His character and his law are our ultimate norms for justice. The difference between equality and equity is clearly discernible in the way God deals with his people. Both the rich and the poor enter into his judgment. Both the rich and the poor are redeemed through the life, death, and resurrection of his Son, Jesus Christ. Our God is both just and merciful, yet he does not shower his material blessings on every man equally. The Promised Land was not divided equally among the twelve tribes. Both Noah and Jacob divided their patriarchal blessings according to the performances of their sons. Reward and punishment are given out according to obedience or disobedience throughout Scripture.

The crux of the debate between advocates of a free economic society and a state-dominated transfer society lies in the definition of justice. The word *justice* has become a catchword that plays a strong emotive role in socialist platforms, while its content dangles in an atmosphere of ambiguity. "Social justice" is a rallying cry that is left undefined. Ronald Nash has done a careful study of the classic meaning of justice in his book *Social Justice and the Christian Church*. He comments on Aristotle's distinction between three kinds of justice: commercial justice, remedial justice, and distributive justice. Nash writes:

(1) Interpersonal relations involving economic exchanges raise questions of *commercial justice*. When people exchange goods and services, questions arise as to whether the exchange is fair or the compensation just. Passages of Scripture like Leviticus 19:36 and Proverbs 16:11 that advise merchants to have just scales and weights seem directed to this type of justice.

(2) Instances where some wrong must be made right under either criminal or civil law are occasions for *remedial justice*. Cases where an innocent individual is found guilty or where the punishment for an offense is too severe or too lenient are instances of injustice in this sense. Exodus 23:3–6 is one of a number of biblical passages that speak to issues of remedial justice.

(3) Finally, questions about *distributive justice* arise in situa-

tions where some good or burden is apportioned among human beings. Such situations are encountered frequently as, for example, when a parent divides the evening dessert among the members of a large family, or a man divides his estate among his heirs. As the term is used in contemporary writings, *social justice* is viewed as that species of distributive justice concerned with the distribution of burdens and benefits within society as a whole, a distribution that is usually controllable by political authorities. [14]

Classical philosophers wrestled with the question of the relationship between justice and human rights. In the Bible, justice is repeatedly linked with the term *righteousness*. Justice is to be given according to righteousness. A "right" is made obligatory by righteousness. The noun *right* can function in different ways. We distinguish, for example, between *legal* rights and *moral* rights. In a perfect society where the laws reflect absolute righteousness, we would expect no discrepancies between moral and legal rights. But such a society does not exist on this planet. Legislatures err, and unjust and unrighteous laws inevitably emerge.

Consider the raging debate in the United States on the abortion issue. One of the repeated claims of advocates of abortion on demand is that "a woman has the right to control her own body." This right includes sovereignty over her own pregnancy. When this claim is made, we must ask, What *kind* of right does the woman have? A legal right? A moral right?

If the claim is simply that a woman has a legal right to abortion and that therefore the present abortion laws ought to remain intact, then the argument is circular. It translates, "I ought to have the right because I have the right." Probably what is meant, however, is that a woman has a *moral* right to control her own body. That is, righteousness demands that a woman be free to terminate a pregnancy if she chooses. But whence cometh this moral right? If God is the ultimate norm of righteousness, a moral right is a God-given right. It is precisely at this point that the abortion advocate is in trouble. God is strangely silent about such moral rights. Indeed,

unless the argument includes a defense of how righteousness demands such a right, the argument is gratuitous. As it stands, it is a
mere declaration, not a reasoned argument.

The term *right* is so emotionally charged in our culture that it
frequently functions as a subterfuge for *personal preference*. A personal desire is translated by linguistic sleight-of-hand into a moral
imperative that must be granted by righteous obligation.

Let us apply this distortion of the word *right* to the economic
arena. Consider the news coverage of steelworkers converging on
the corporate headquarters of U.S. Steel. The company has just
announced the shut-down of another large mill with the resulting
lay-off of hundreds of workers. The unemployed steelworkers picket
the corporate headquarters with placards proclaiming their right to
remain employed. In interviews spokesmen angrily demand that
the company restore their rightful jobs. Spokesmen for the company
defend the closing of the mill on the grounds that it is losing money.
U.S. Steel, they argue, is in business to make a profit.

Does a company have the moral obligation to provide jobs if the
company is losing money? Conversely, does a human being have
an inalienable right to be employed? Does every American have an
intrinsic right to a job? We know that God imposes a moral obligation on people to work. Does that obligation to work at the same
time impose an obligation on someone else to provide the job? I
trust the answer is self-evident. I am responsible to work, but my
obligation to work does not imply either logically or morally that
someone else has the obligation to employ me. Employment is a
trade agreement whereby both parties profit. I sell my labor for
wages. If my labor is not desired, no one has an obligation to employ
me.

What, then, is justice? Nash relates justice to *a person's due*:

> The ancients believed that justice always involves giving a
> person his due, that to which he has a right. The reason why
> a person may be due something varies with his or her situa-
> tion. A hypothetical person named Jones would be due some-
> thing in each of the following cases:

(1) If Jones does better work than any other student in the class, she is due the best grade.

(2) If Jones is the prettiest contestant in a beauty contest, she is due first prize.

(3) If Jones is the first to finish a race, she is due the prize.

(4) If Jones is promised something by Smith, Jones is due the fulfillment of that promise.

(5) If Jones' property is stolen or damaged by Smith, Jones is due whatever reparation is required to restore what she lost.

The what and the why of any person's due cannot be reduced to a single formula. . . . However much the determination of a person's due varies with the situation, it seems clear that the essence of justice involves each person having or receiving that which he is due. At the very least, justice occurs in situations where people receive what they are due. In any case where someone is denied what he or she is due, an injustice has occurred. [15]

Socialism distorts justice. The fruits of one man's labor are given to another, in the interest of equality at the expense of equity. The poor man is assumed to have the right to the wealth of another man. The wealthy man loses his right to the fruit of his own labor. Under a socialist economy the poor are not lifted up to produce equality, but the wealthy are brought down. Socialism breeds an unjust bias against the wealthy, making them the target of public scorn and inequitable taxation. It is difficult to generate sympathy for the wealthy. Their wealth provides them with so many advantages, so many luxuries, so much power, that it is easy for the envious to assume that they can afford injustice. Media images frequently depict the rich as unscrupulous, pompous, foolish, wasteful, bigoted, and uncaring. The J. R. Ewings of this world capture the fancy of the public, justifying hatred for the rich.

This caricature of the rich is unjust. Equity calls for truth in the way we look at people. The biblical call to equity is a call to understanding, to being open and loving to members of all other political and economic camps. Equity is essential to a just and prosperous nation.

The dream of an egalitarian society made possible by coercive policies of transfer or redistribution of wealth is not only unjust, but also ineffective. It has been argued that free enterprise gives out uneven slices of the doughnut and that socialism gives out equal portions of the hole. This aphorism has in view the trend in redistributionist societies toward a net loss in national wealth. Transfer societies penalize achievement and subsidize inefficiency. Where free competition tends toward excellence and increased production, the policies of transfer encourage dependence on government subsidies and a dehumanizing addiction to welfare. The builder, the entrepreneur, the superproducer are stifled by government intervention.

The United States represented, in its inception, a political and economic experiment. The nation was built on a system of free enterprise. Economic freedom was viewed as an essential to political freedom. Freedom was understood to involve free exchange in the marketplace, freedom to produce, and freedom to enjoy the fruits of one's production. But a watershed economic crisis led to the redefinition of freedom. The aftermath of the Great Depression left a hunger for freedom from want and insecurity. Government intervention became the order of the day as Keynesian theory became a political and economic reality.

The Great Depression was nearly the downfall of our free enterprise system. Citizens began to doubt the market system. They were convinced that it had failed, causing raging unemployment, home foreclosures, bank closings, and hunger. With only 150 years of history behind it, the nation was now hesitant to continue the grand experiment.

The New Deal effort to restore the collapsing economy brought unprecedented levels of government regulation, taxation, and inflationary policies. Government began to mushroom through the creation of new federal agencies. This was not viewed as a repudiation of free-market economics, but as a necessary adjustment to see the nation through a crisis in a boom–bust cycle.

The post-Depression adjustment turned out not to be temporary.

The new policies and new definition of freedom created new expectations. The principle of limited government with limited involvement in the marketplace was gradually lost in the political race to win more votes with promises of greater government benefits. Slowly, but inexorably, the transition to a transfer society set in. In 1960, federal, state, and local expenditures on social welfare programs totaled $52 billion. In 1965 the figure reached $77.2 billion. In 1975 these expenditures equaled $286 billion.[16]

There is still a margin of free enterprise in the United States, but that margin is rapidly shrinking to the diminishing point. We live in a nation of increasing wealth transfer. Socialism as an economic policy is no longer creeping; it is up and running. The federal government is by far the nation's largest employer. Imagine for a moment the sheer magnitude of a government that has a $200-billion deficit. The amount of power now held by the state is so immense that it is virtually unfathomable.

The folly of replacing equity with equality is perilous to the nation's economy. A system based on redistribution leads to economic and political horror. Soviet history makes this point vividly. The failures of the Soviet economy are not due to a failure in applying Marx's ideals. They are due to the country's success in applying them. Under socialism, the rich get poorer and the poor get poorer. Under capitalism, the rich get richer and the poor get richer. Equity tends to prosperity; equality tends to poverty.

The paycheck we bring home is our profit. We trade our skills for our wages. Let us assume that our skills are in great demand, so our profit is substantial. Someone else, a person of low skills, brings home very little profit because his skills are not in great demand. The beneficent government, seeing the gross inequality of income between us, steps in with the graduated income tax. The second man is put on the rolls of four or five government programs. Money is redistributed, and we are now on a relatively equal plane of wealth, or poverty, depending upon whether we see the cup as half full or half empty.

When profit is destroyed through redistribution, so also is the national wealth. Not only is the high-profit taxpayer hurt, but the recipients of equality-producing programs are hurt also. Profit is the first of our five ingredients for material prosperity. When profit goes, so goes material prosperity. Money taken by the government cannot be invested privately. Without that private investment, the poor man's skills will remain in low demand as industries shut down and unemployment rises. Government programs designed to make the country more equal only hurt the entire nation.

Profit is the goose that lays the golden eggs. It provides incentive to work, it allows for investment, and it is the basis for all trade. Killing the goose to divide it equally among our citizens may provide us with one glorious banquet today, but it ensures starvation tomorrow. The goose is strangled and lays eggs no more. As long as profit is taxed away in the name of equality, the goose can lay no more golden eggs. There is no incentive, and there is no capital for future investment.

The destruction of our national wealth will continue as long as there are those who can sell equality. To legislators and bureaucrats, the death of the golden goose is a blessing. Those in power who proclaim their hopes and plans for the end of poverty are the very persons who benefit from its continuation. An end of poverty would be the end of jobs for those who sell the economics of equality. Politicians step onto their soapboxes, promising more and more government money for poverty programs. The programs are born, profit is taxed, poverty grows, new programs are formed, more profits are taxed, and more people are poor. The process goes on and on. The welfare rolls swell, and the votes pour in for the humanitarian politicians who promise the most programs. These pimps of poverty make their living by making more people poor and then promising to help them with more poverty-inducing programs. The cycle goes on and on as the goose is gasping for breath. The more the goose falters, the more the poor will line up to vote for their newest savior. Politicians thrive on the failures of their own bad economic systems as their promises grow to newer heights. In 1983, entitlement dollars spent for program administration—chiefly for the salaries of government employees—averaged $35,000 per person on welfare, a sum equal to three times the poverty level of income. The tragedy is that the purchasing power of the dollar owned by the poor man is diminished precisely by the programs designed to aid him.

Christians often bring up the year of Jubilee as a defense for the policy of redistribution. But the year of Jubilee was not a policy of redistribution of wealth. Rather it was an early example of the renting of property. Leviticus 25:11–16 tells how the year of Jubilee was to work:

> The fiftieth year shall be a jubilee for you; do not sow and do not reap what grows of itself or harvest the untended vines. For it is a jubilee and is to be holy for you; eat only what is taken directly from the fields. In this Year of Jubilee everyone is to return to his own property. If you sell land to one of your countrymen or buy any from him, do not take advantage of each other. You are to buy from your countryman on the basis of the number of years since the Jubilee. And he is to sell to you on the basis of the number of years left for harvesting crops. When the years are many, you are to increase the price, and when the years are few, you are to decrease the price, because what he is really selling you is the number of crops. [NIV]

Jubilee was not a program of redistribution. No masses were counting down the years until they could reclaim what some unethical corporation had taken from them. The idea behind Jubilee was to make the inheritance, the Promised Land, permanent and at the same time productive. Its intention was to protect private property, not abolish it. If a man had ten daughters and one son, he had difficulty farming his land. If another man had ten sons, he was able to farm his own land and more. The man with many daughters rented his land to the man with many sons. The fifty-year period of Jubilee allowed for the passing of generations so that families could start over. The land was eventually restored to its original owner, but the renter was allowed to keep profits he made while farming it. No coercive transfer mechanism was involved. Jubilee allowed for the free market to work in the Promised Land.

NINE
GOVERNMENT FORCE AND PERSONAL FREEDOM

Government is force. This equation is so elementary that it is easily obscured in the complexities of theories of government. We tend to think of force in purely negative terms, associating it with a particular form of government, tyranny. Yet it is vital for us to realize that all government, by its very nature, involves establishing a legalized system of force.

Government is force whether its form is monarchy, totalitarianism, or democracy. It is easy to think that in a free democratic society government is not force. Democracy bases its existence on the consent of the governed. Government leaders come into office through elections, not bloody coups; laws are passed through free legislative action moderated by various types of checks and balances; taxes are paid freely, without confiscation.

What remains obscured by political rhetoric is that even in a free society where democratic government is based on the consent of the governed, what the governed consent to is to be governed by force. An official is elected to an authority role backed up by force. Violations of laws enacted in a free society are met by force: arrest or detention. If the taxpayer refuses to pay his taxes, his taxes will be confiscated.

Recently a prominent United States senator made the casual remark at lunch in the Senate dining room, "I do not believe the government ever has the right to coerce anyone to do anything."

The statement was astonishing. If taken literally, it could only mean that no government ever has the right to govern. Without coercion the government has no means of law enforcement. Enforcement, as the root of the word indicates, involves force. Its power is limited to offering suggestions. At best it can counsel or advise its citizens to behave in certain ways. In such a schema, taxes would have to be turned into free-will offerings.

Force, of course, is a general term, a genus with a wide variety of species. There are different kinds, different levels, different degrees of force. Police brutality, for example, is a kind of excessive force. It is an abuse of the right of coercion. Obviously force can be misused to inflict injustice upon people. A misuse of parental force results in child abuse. A misuse of national government force results in oppression. There may be a big difference in the ways a democracy and a dictatorship use force, but we must keep in mind that both are governments and therefore both use force.

The word *force* is so loaded with negative connotations that it may be difficult for us to be comfortable with the idea that it is not intrinsically bad. The Christian must keep in mind that government is ordained and instituted by God. Government was established even before the fall of man. Adam and Eve were made governors over creation. In turn they were created under government, under the rule of God. When they transgressed against their Creator, they were forced to leave Eden. After their expulsion from the garden, God appointed an angel with a flaming sword to stand guard at the entrance to Eden lest Adam seek to force his way back to paradise. "So he drove out the man; and he placed at the east of the garden of Eden Cherubims, and a flaming sword which turned every way, to keep the way of the tree of life" (Gen. 3:24).

Augustine argued that government is not so much a necessary evil as an institution made necessary by evil. It is because of sin that human government is necessary. Sin is a destructive force by which we violate other people and violate nature itself. The principal purpose of government is to restrain evil.

Theology must always include a vital concern about government. The giants of Christian theology have all concerned themselves with the role of civil government under the sovereign authority of God.

Concerned about questions of what constitutes a just and legitimate government, they faced the political issues of their time with no less zeal than the liberation theologians of our own day.

Augustine, for example, was concerned with the role of government in protecting human happiness. He stressed that happiness is ultimately rooted in a proper relationship with God, but recognized at the same time that human happiness can be thwarted by crimes committed against us. When my family is victimized by theft or murder, when I am defrauded in my business enterprises, my pursuit of happiness is frustrated. The role of government is to restrain those evil forces that rob people of happiness in this world.

Martin Luther's work in the area of political theory has been the occasion of controversy. Luther has been credited with everything from being the forerunner of Hegel and totalitarian fascism to being a prime architect of the principle of separation of church and state. Whatever the case, Luther certainly maintained that the secular state was divinely ordered, and he stressed the duty of God-fearing citizens to fulfill their obligations of civil obedience.

John Calvin followed in the tradition of Augustine and Luther in his support of civil government as a divine institution. Calvin, like the others, took his point of departure from the pivotal New Testament teaching on the state:

> Let every soul be subject unto the higher powers. For there is no power but of God: the powers that be are ordained of God. Whosoever therefore resisteth the power, resisteth the ordinance of God; and they that resist shall receive to themselves damnation. For rulers are not a terror to good works, but to the evil. Wilt thou then not be afraid of the power? do that which is good, and thou shalt have praise of the same: for he is the minister of God to thee for good. But if thou do that which is evil, be afraid; for he beareth not the sword in vain: for he is the minister of God, a revenger to execute wrath upon him that doeth evil. Wherefore ye must needs be subject, not only for wrath, but also for conscience sake. For for this cause pay ye tribute also: for they are God's ministers, attending continually upon this very thing. Render therefore to all their

dues; tribute to whom tribute is due; custom to whom custom; fear to whom fear; honour to whom honour. [Rom. 13:1–7]

The apostle Peter echoes Paul's teaching:

Submit yourselves to every ordinance of man for the Lord's sake: whether it be to the king, as supreme; or unto governors, as unto them that are sent by him for the punishment of evildoers, and for the praise of them that do well, for so is the will of God, that with well doing ye may put to silence the ignorance of foolish men: as free, and not using your liberty for a cloke of maliciousness, but as the servants of God. Honour all men. Love the brotherhood. Fear God. Honour the king. [1 Pet. 2:13–17]

In these classic passages we hear a strong admonition to the Christian to render respectful civil obedience. These passages make it virtually impossible for a Christian to embrace anarchy. Yet the stress on civil obedience does not mean that the Christian may never disobey the government. There are times when the Christian citizen not only may, but must, disobey civil authorities. The circumstances for justifiable civil disobedience will be explored later. First we must seek to understand the biblical stress on positive obedience.

Peter's statement that we are to submit ourselves to the authorities for "the Lord's sake" helps us understand why civil obedience is imperative. The kingdom of God is, in a very real sense, a political structure. It involves the seat of cosmic governing authority. The title ascribed to Jesus, "King of Kings and Lord of Lords," not only is an exercise in laudatory expression but is rooted in concrete reality. All authority in heaven and in earth has been given by God the Father to God the Son. Christ is established at the right hand of God as the supreme governor of the universe. All lesser authorities are subject to him. If this were not so, then the biblical confession of the lordship of Christ would be empty of meaning.

Wanton disobedience of or disrespect toward earthly authorities reflects on the authority that stands over and above them. To have a cavalier attitude toward the local dogcatcher is to insult the majesty of Christ to whom the dogcatcher is ultimately accountable. A sin against the earthly authority is a sin against the cosmic crown adorning the head of Christ.

New Testament injunctions about civil obedience are responding to the worldwide problem of lawlessness. Evil is not merely a local, isolated, particular phenomenon. Every act of wickedness ripples out from its center to spill over a wide area of life. Every sin we commit is an act of lawlessness against God and adds to the total complex of evil. Every human being participates in this complex. Our fallen nature is given to lawlessness. The supreme, quintessential representative of all evil is called "the man of lawlessness" (2 Thess. 2:3, NIV). It is not strange that the New Testament is somber in its warnings to be scrupulous in our obedience to authority. The spirit of lawlessness lurks behind our every sin.

We have said that in spite of the strong admonitions to civil obedience that we find in the New Testament there are occasions when the Christian not only may but must disobey the civil authorities. The principle that guides us in this issue is both simple and clear: we are called to disobey the civil authorities whenever they command us to do something God forbids or forbid us to do something that God commands. If obedience to the civil authorities entails disobedience to God, we must obey God rather than men. If the civil authority commands us to steal or to murder, we must disobey. If the civil authority forbids the preaching of the gospel, we must nevertheless continue to preach the gospel.

What if civil laws inconvenience me or oppress me? Here the applications become excruciatingly difficult. To disobey the speed limit merely because it inconveniences me is to add to the complex of lawlessness. But if the government oppresses us—if it, for example, imposes an oppressive tax burden—are we called to docile compliance? Here students of Christian ethics disagree. On the one hand, the Bible clearly tells us to pay our taxes. The New Testament gives such instructions in the context of the Roman Empire, which placed a heavy tax burden upon the Jews. To some Christians, there is thus little room for argument about the Christian's duty to pay his taxes. He may protest oppressive tax burdens by speaking out against them or by marching in a peaceful, nonviolent demonstration in front of the White House or the Internal Revenue Service. But in the meantime, he must keep paying his taxes. Other Christians, however, argue to the contrary. They focus on the biblical instruction to pay our taxes to those to whom taxes are due (see Mt. 22:21; Rom. 13:7). The issue is then whether unjust taxes are ever due anyone. Obviously, it is not always easy to know how to apply the straightforward biblical principle on civil disobedience.

The Christian faces a dilemma: civil governments, though ordained by God, can nevertheless become demonized. They can become instruments of terror, injustice, oppression, and wickedness. Instead of promoting the general peace, they can promote violence. Instead of safeguarding the sanctity of life, they can destroy it either directly or by permissive legislation as in the case of legalized abortion. Instead of protecting private property, they may become the very instruments used to steal, confiscate, or redistribute it.

God gives civil governments the "power of the sword." With that power comes the responsibility to use the sword in the cause of justice. When civil magistrates use the sword as an instrument of injustice, they not only are doing violence to their victims, but are also rebelling against God and his Christ. The government's right to the sword is always circumscribed by its responsibility to use it judiciously. When the sword is used unjustly, the government has degenerated into tyranny.

The primary use of the sword is to protect, sustain, and maintain life. The government is called to restrain and punish those who would take the life of another by murder. The sword is to be used to defend the lives of the innocent and to punish the guilty, whether an aggressor nation or an individual murderer.

The second responsibility of the government is to protect private property. The government may use forcible restraint to prevent robbery or vandalism. This responsibility goes beyond matters of direct and outright theft. Fraud in the marketplace violates private property rights, and the government should work to prevent it.

These twin roles of government, protecting life and protecting property, are both intended to preserve freedom. Government force is to be used to restrain other forces that would violate personal life and property. When the government itself uses force to violate life and property, it becomes the criminal it has been ordained to restrain.

Liberty is the central and crucial principle in the American dream of democracy. Freedom has been the most celebrated virtue in our national heritage. The Constitution promises our citizens the rights to life, liberty, and the pursuit of happiness. Our Pledge of Allegiance declares that we stand for liberty and justice for all. Our national anthem calls America the "land of the free." Freedom is our heritage, won by the blood of our fathers and guaranteed by our Constitution.

In the thirties, as a result of the economic upheaval of the Great Depression, a subtle but powerful change in the meaning of freedom emerged in our culture. Under the New Deal, President Roosevelt introduced a new concept of freedom: freedom from want. Freedom from want became a new ideal that made it acceptable to compromise classical rights. The government stepped in to free people from poverty and financial insecurity, enacting new measures to secure economic security. Unfortunately, such guarantees necessitated programs aimed at redistributing wealth. The poor were now "entitled" to a certain level of financial security, even if it required the use of government force to impose unjust taxation on the wealthy. The government embraced a legalized Robin Hood policy.

This new definition of freedom had no historical precedent. In Europe, freedom historically was equated with local national government; it meant first of all that a country would not be ruled by a foreign power. France was "free" under the emperor Napoleon since no foreign power controlled the government. The American concept went further. Here freedom meant that no government, including our own, would interfere unnecessarily in the lives of the citizens. This freedom was guaranteed by the power of the vote; private citizens could now help form policies with all the power of government force behind them. Paradoxically, the power to vote can destroy freedom as well as guarantee it, if voters enact their own special interests without regard to justice and righteousness. The use of government force to enhance special interests, without regard to the rights of the minority, is an abomination to God. The Christian may not exercise his right to vote as an instrument to steal from other people.

But surely Christians don't ever do this, do they? Every day in a multitude of ways! The Christian who votes for measures that will subsidize his business is using his ballot to take money from someone else to underwrite his program. The parent who applies for a government loan to pay his child's education is using government force to take money from some private individual to pay for his child's education. Most Christians wouldn't think of going to their neighbors with a gun and demanding payment for their child's college education. But they will vote for such entitlements, forgetting that someone must be standing at their neighbors' door with a gun to insure the tax dollars will be there to provide for the college loan.

With the redefinition of freedom as freedom from want, the government has undertaken a new series of responsibilities. Today our citizens expect the government to provide for their economic security. They assume that it is the government's responsibility to insure the success of their businesses. Farmers march on Washington demanding price floors, parity programs, and other forms of subsidization. Unemployed laborers demand jobs or job-training programs. Business executives demand more tariffs and trade barriers. Scientists and artists clamor for money for their research and cultural enrichment programs. Traditionally the artist has depended upon the voluntary patronage of those who saw the cultural value of his contribution. Public television programs still solicit funds through charitable contributions, but the trend is toward finding support not through private donations but through government grants.

The new freedom, freedom from want, finds our government using its sword to cut cheese and butter and to turn over crops. The sword guards our borders not so much from the invasion of foreign armies as from the invasion of foreign autos, steel, and electronics.

As our wants grow, so grows the government. There is no ceiling to all of our possible wants, so a government promising freedom from want has a big job to do. It is not strange that since freedom has been redefined the growth of government has been exponential. But as government grows, our freedom fades proportionately. With each new government power comes an automatic and irresistible loss of private freedom. The Constitutional system of checks and balances that was designed to retard growth in government power is no longer able to do that effectively.

Most of our citizens seem not to fear the loss of economic freedom. The carrot of economic security has been too appealing. They apparently assume that as long as our political freedom is intact there is no need to fear the loss of economic freedom. This fallacy is as deadly as it is seductive. Economic and political liberty may be distinguished but never separated. They are bound up with each other.

Consider, for example, the freedom of the press. Soviet Russia has no laws governing what the press may or may not write. The Soviet constitution guarantees freedom of the press, but all legal Soviet printing presses are owned by the government. As a result nothing bad is said about the Russian government. With no economic freedom of the press, there can be no political freedom of the press either.

At the present moment there is no widespread protest in America about the loss of political and economic freedom. If the erosion of liberty that has taken place gradually over the past fifty years had happened suddenly and dramatically, there would undoubtedly have been riots in the streets and a call to arms. But the gradualism of the change has left us much like the proverbial frog who is warmed so slowly that in his lethargy he fails to jump out of the pan before the water boils. We have a national sense of security and well-being about living in a democracy rather than behind the Iron Curtain. We see the obvious differences between the methods of force employed in Communist countries and those used in socialist countries. Communist rulers tend to kill their way into power while socialists use the ballot box. Socialist nations do not build walls to keep their citizens captive and secret police activities are not routine. But lest we view these differences from a Pollyanna perspective, we must keep in mind that the ballot is a bullet. Laws established by vote carry no less force behind them than the decrees of a dictator. The dictator's guns fire the same kind of bullets as the guns used by law enforcement agencies of democratic nations. Both political structures make abundant use of prisons. Tyranny can exist in either style of government.

The year that the American Revolution began saw also the publication of Adam Smith's *Wealth of Nations*. New advances were made in the understanding of economics as a science.

More than thirty years before in France, Montesquieu's landmark work, *The Spirit of Laws*, set forth the thesis that there are basically only three types of government: dictatorships, monarchies, and democracies. Through historical induction, he tried to discover the distinguishing characteristics of each of these forms.

In dictatorships, Montesquieu reasoned *fear* is the indispensable element of continuity. That is, the dictator depends upon the power of fear to keep his subjects paralyzed. Bloody purges and secret police action are the dictator's necessary tools if he is to keep his power. If the populace ever overcomes their fear enough to rise up against him, the dictator is threatened. No dictator can afford a Lech Walesa running around loose in his domain.

Monarchy does not rest on fear. Its chief necessary factor for continuity is *honor*. The social structure of lords and ladies, the pomp and circumstance of regal ceremony, the elaborate costumes (regalia) of the ruling bodies are all vital to maintaining a cultural milieu in which a monarchy can flourish. The word *courtesy* derives from the word *court*; it describes the behavior appropriate around royalty. The touchstone of courtesy is honor. The ruffian who knows no courtesy, who eschews honor, is the figure who represents the greatest threat to monarchy.

In his analysis of democracy, Montesquieu singled out *civic righteousness* as the absolute prerequisite for the survival of the system. He understood the power of the ballot and the potential problems created by the tyranny of the majority. The laws of a free society must reflect righteousness rather than special interest if the democracy is to survive.

Montesquieu further argued that if one of the above systems collapses, it is usually replaced by one of the other two. Monarchy is not a great threat nowadays, but if democracy collapses for want of civic righteousness, what is to prevent its being replaced by dictatorship?

Similar warnings were issued in the nineteenth century by Alexis de Tocqueville. He warned that two great threats hovered over the nascent American republic. The first was that people would discover that the vote was worth money. That is, the potential for bribery, graft, and political corruption is built into any system that involves courting votes as a necessary stepping stone to power. The second great threat was that people might vote themselves largesse. Once people discovered that they could use the government to enrich themselves, the seeds of the destruction of democracy would be sown. The most crucial safeguard against both of these threats was the law.

Since the time of ancient Greece, the most vital ingredient to a free society has been found in its lawcode. According to Frédéric Bastiat the final issue determining the survival of a free society is whether it is ruled by law or by men. This point is as critical as it is difficult to protect from confusion.

At first glance the terms *rule by law* and *rule by men* seem to be a distinction without a difference. Is it not true that in a democratic society laws are made by men? The legislative bodies are composed of neither gods nor angels. Men enact the laws and men compose constitutions. Jefferson and Franklin were both mortals. Washington was from Virginia, not Mt. Olympus. How then can Bastiat distinguish between rule by men and rule by law?

When the American republic was formed, there was a consensus that a nation's laws should be established upon some sort of higher law, a law transcending the interpretations and vested interests of individuals or groups. The higher law to which Jeffersonian democracy appealed was the *lex natura*, the law of nature. Philosophers, from Cicero and the Stoics down through the formers of British lawcodes, held that nature itself mirrors an ultimate law, the *lex supernaturalis*. However they stated their belief, Christians, Jews, deists, and humanists all sought an objective foundation for law, a foundation that would insure that Lady Justice's blindfold did not slip.

The breakdown of natural law as an objective safeguard to rule by men was hastened by the philosophical influence of American pragmatism. The thinking of William James, John Dewey, and

Franklin Pierce built on Immanuel Kant's skepticism of man's ability to know anything of a transcendent nature. If God is unknowable to the human mind, then it follows that his transcendent Law is equally unknowable. Once the foundation for the *lex aeternitatis* was attacked, the *lex naturalis* was left hanging in midair. Only a short time after Kant, the relevance of natural law to their area of concern was rejected by the majority of students of jurisprudence, so that today natural law is treated rarely, if ever, in American law schools. When Oliver Wendell Holmes became the chief justice of the Supreme Court, he implemented a radically new philosophy of law. In his classic work on common law, Holmes declared that laws cannot reflect some nebulous transcendent norm of religious or philosophical truth, but must always reflect the desires of the contemporary community. Here is the clearest expression of rule by men that can be found in the annals of American jurisprudence. Holmes's work was a watershed marking the transition from rule by law to rule by men. This transition is substantive and dramatic, as it gives license to the tyranny of the majority.

The fruit of legal pragmatism is called *law positivism*. Law positivism simply means that particular laws are all we ultimately have. There are no transcendent norms. There is no absolute law. In this schema it is possible always and ever to reinterpret the Constitution to bring its application into conformity with current community standards. Current community standards, of course, can support pornography, abortion, and a host of other highly controversial legal issues. The meaning of the phrase is simple: whatever the majority desires becomes law. In effect the Constitution's posture as the supreme sentinel for rule by law is broken and bent.

TEN
WHERE ARE WE HEADED?

The American economy is suffering from a growing rate of taxation brought about in large part by the explosive growth of government and government spending. The federal deficit is increasing yearly. By 1983 the federal budget climbed to $800 billion—an astronomical amount of money. To help get a handle on the meaning of that amount of money, suppose that the day Christ was born you had $800 billion to spend (without the benefit of daily compounded interest). You set about spending the principal at a rate of $1 million a day. If you spent $1 million a day every day since Jesus was born, by 2000 you would still have nearly $70 billion left to spend.

The growth of government can be seen in the fact that the current annual deficit is larger than the entire annual budget was during the Johnson administration's Great Society. From the start of the Carter administration to the first year of the Reagan administration, the annual deficit quadrupled.

In 1983 the federal debt (accumulated deficit) climbed over $1 trillion. The debt represents the amount of money the government needs—but does not have—to pay its bills.

For every fiscal year, the president makes a projected budget. This must be approved by Congress. Each year the amount of money the government spends increases, as does the amount of money the government takes. Spending, however, is climbing at a faster rate than income. This is the cause of the deficit. It is customary for the president to promise a balanced budget. This has not been achieved in over twenty years, and prospects for the immediate future are grim. Deficits will probably go higher in the future as budgets bear the burden of keeping "freedom from want" alive, and as the government faces the interest on a $1-trillion debt. The load of a mounting interest payment makes escape from deficit extremely problematic.

The federal government has only two sources of income. The government does not produce; it does not trade; it does not profit. Every dollar the government spends, whether it be for a welfare mother, a jobs program, or a B-1 bomber, it must first take from the private sector. The government has nothing to give by itself; it must first take before it can give.

The government has two primary sources of income: taxation and printing fiat money. Issuing bonds is not a real source of income because it amounts to the government's promise to tax or print in the future. Bonds are merely loans the government takes out on the American people. The interest and the principal are later paid by the citizens.

Projected income is the amount of money the government expects to take in during any given year. Taxation, equal to approximately 30 percent of the gross national product, is not enough to cover a year's projected and real spending. The difference is the deficit, which the government reduces by printing fiat money. The government issues an order to the Federal Reserve for funds to cover the deficit. The funds are delivered via the printing press. This inflationary action is the government's second source of income, and it causes at least as much of a problem as the ballooning taxation. As we have seen, inflation devalues the currency. Its net effect on the taxpayer is to reduce his purchasing power as much as or more than if the government had simply increased taxes to a higher rate. It can hurt the taxpayer more by virtue of "bracket creep": the wage earner's inflated earnings put him into a higher tax bracket even though they do not increase his real purchasing power.

The government can only tax so much: wage earners know why their take-home pay is so much less than their gross income. But those who complain about their taxes can usually be counted on to clamor for more government programs that will put government money into their pockets. Politicians cannot afford to alienate the legions of voters who want less taxation and more programs. The political solution to this dilemma is deficit spending backed by an increased money supply, but this is a vicious circle. The loss of purchasing power due to a 30 percent increase in the money supply is much more difficult to see than the loss due to withheld taxes, but it is as real and painful.

Deficit spending works as long as the voting public remains ignorant of the true nature of inflation. As long as inflation is seen as a business problem or an entity with a life all its own, the government will be tempted to continue inflationary policies. They have our blessing to discourage saving, hinder capital investment, and otherwise take the vitality out of our national economy. The blame for inflation rests both on the shoulders of our government leaders and on the public who demand political promises from their candidates.

Special-interest groups play a significant role in deficit spending. A special-interest group is a block of voters who feel strongly about one issue and want government money for it. In exchange for votes and monetary support, a candidate for public office will agree to promote the special interest. These groups range in size from small medical research groups to the National Education Association with its 1.7 million members. The NEA threw its support and money behind presidential hopeful Jimmy Carter during the 1976 presidential campaign, and once in office Carter created a new cabinet-level department, the Department of Education.

Special-interest activity, in fulfillment of Alexis de Tocqueville's prophecy that democracy will work until people realize they can vote themselves largesse, pushes up government spending to newer heights, making deficit spending a political necessity. The price tag is staggering.

The government also runs up a large bill in support of private businesses. Low-interest loans to private businesses run the budget still higher. Business welfare is growing while the welfare of business is declining due to high taxes and an inflated money supply. From funding the continental railroad to setting up satellites, the government is deep in the business of business. This unholy alliance distorts the market system and costs the taxpayer dearly.

Government intervention in the farming industry also costs the taxpayer. Rather than allowing farm products to be sold through free interaction between supply and demand, the government sets price floors. These artificially high prices dry up demand for the products. The resulting surplus is bought up by the government, driving up the budget once more.

The government is also in the business of funding incompetence. In the interest of antimonopoly sentiments and misled patriotic feelings, the government spends billions trying to revive dead or dying industries. The Chrysler Corporation is the third largest manufacturer of cars in the United States. A few years ago it stood on the brink of bankruptcy. It was losing a great deal of money year after year, because the public did not prefer its products in a competitive market. Most businesses that cannot sell their product, like Braniff Airlines, go out of business. This was not the fate of the Chrysler Corporation. They received a generous low-interest loan of $1.5 billion from our government. You and I and Henry Ford III—America's taxpayers—were forced to finance this bail-out. Chrysler received $1.5 billion that could have been used by productive businesses that met the needs of the public. Had the money been left in the marketplace, it could have provided jobs for strong businesses. The loan did not save jobs; it merely transfered them. We must keep in mind that government can only give that which it first takes.

The government has other means besides low-interest loans and grants to protect and aid incompetent industries. The tariff has long been used in America not as a means of raising revenue, but rather to protect weak domestic industries. Protective tariffs are a problem to every consumer in America. The fallacy of the protective tariff is an old one, one that Adam Smith refuted over two hundred years ago in *The Wealth of Nations*. Smith wrote:

> In every country it always is and must be the interest of the great body of the people to buy whatever they want of those who sell it cheapest. The proposition is so very manifest that

it seems ridiculous to take any pains to prove it; nor could it ever have been called in question, had not the interested sophistry of merchants and manufacturers confounded the common sense of mankind.[17]

Harley-Davidson is the last remaining producer of motorcycles in America. They have not built a better or cheaper motorcycle than their foreign competitors. Let us assume that their only model costs $1,500, and that a Japanese manufacturer can sell a motorcycle of the same quality for $1,250. Harley-Davidson would be out of business without a tariff, leaving workers unemployed. The government charges the Japanese producers $250 to sell their product in America. On the surface it appears that many American jobs are saved by the tariff. Or are they?

Let us assume that our government removes the tariff. Harley-Davidson goes out of business. Those who buy motorcycles now have 250 more dollars to spend elsewhere. This may mean one more job in one factory, or two in another. This money will create jobs, productive jobs in competent businesses. In addition, the Japanese manufacturer will eventually spend his American dollars in America on businesses that are competent, that can produce something cheap and in demand, unlike Harley-Davidson. Ultimately tariffs save no jobs, and they cost the consumer. They benefit only the noncompetitive business. The government cannot save one industry without in turn hurting hundreds of others.

The government is likewise guilty of costing the public billions of dollars annually through its practice of price-fixing. Price-fixing disrupts the basic components of the free market: supply and demand.

Upon entering the marketplace, every consumer and producer arrives with their own value system. As with the bubble gum and baseball cards, transactions work best when left unhampered.

A roadside corn seller may wish to charge $2.25 a bushel for his corn. But to no avail: consumers are unwilling to spend that much on corn.

The government can attempt to impose values on the citizens, but such attempts will always backfire. Economic value is subjective and therefore not subject to government decrees. The government can force the bubble gum seller to set a price, but it cannot force him to *value* his bubble gum less than he does or a consumer to value it more.

WHERE DO WE GO FROM HERE?

Economics, the dismal science, rarely gives its students the opportunity to rejoice over new discoveries. The physicist who comes to a better understanding of electricity is able to contribute to a better light bulb. The chemist is able to produce a vaccine to aid in world health. The biologist may help develop a new high-protein grain. Economists enjoy no such discoveries.

Alvin Toffler's best-selling book *The Third Wave* predicts a bright future for the world, based on technological advancements. Applied science will bring the world more and better food, more jobs, and increasing prosperity. Others predict cancer cures, better crop yields, and better light bulbs. Economists of all sorts, however— liberals, conservatives, and moderates—predict only economic problems. Liberals predict that any conservative tilt to an administration's economic policy will lead directly to economic disaster. At the same time conservative economists attack the liberal aspects of the same administration's policy. Everyone hopes to gain prestige from predicting economic downfall, knowing that if the economy grows stronger no one worries about false predictions. It is not the science of economics that is dismal; it is the economists themselves.

This book has examined the biblical principles that guide any proper study of economics. We have observed the dynamics of economic interaction, the tools necessary for economic prosperity, the relationship of supply and demand, the evolution of trade and money, the nature of profit, and the nature of government. We have seen the many ways the American government and governments abroad have wrongfully interfered with economic processes. We have examined some of the follies that the government commits every day. We have looked at destructive attitudes people have toward trade, profit, and saving.

When confronted with our present state of economic affairs, we must plan to avert these problems in the future. Many want to know what can be done to stop the tide of increasing government spending, redistribution programs, inflation, and regulation. As Christians, we are in a delicate position: it is our duty to obey the government. We may not cheat on tax forms to protect what is rightfully ours. We may not disobey government regulations, no matter how destructive they may be. What can we do?

The first step in stopping government growth is *not to use* government services. We pay our taxes, and many of us wish to get our money back. So we send our children to public schools; allow the government to finance our loans on college education, houses, and business improvements; and buy government bonds. All this, if the government is to be held in check, must stop. Anyone dedicated to small government must stop using the government for his own personal gain.

Some hope to gain revenge against the government by collecting as many government dollars as possible. This revenge ultimately is paid for by other taxpayers and not by the government. Any money the government takes from you is gone, spent. Anything you receive, beyond protection of life and property, is taken from another unjustly. To stop incessant taxing and spending we must adopt a cheek-turning policy, and not one of an eye for an eye.

To illustrate, let's examine the social security program. Those dollars which the government takes for your future are not for your future but for someone else's present. Your monthly social security payment is spent by the time you pay the next month's payment. The government is not putting your money away in a bank account until you retire. The money goes to Washington to pay the salaries of the army of bureaucrats who run the system. What is left is quickly passed on to retirees across the nation. The money is gone. If you retire and receive social security, those who pay for it are those still working. Social security is not a program of mandatory saving for old age; it is a program of the young subsidizing the old.

If no one accepted government money, the federal budget would shrink to a reasonable size. We must avoid an attitude that "if I don't take it, someone else will." We can effectively boycott government spending programs, thus lowering taxation and inflation as well as improving the economy. Accepting wealth-transfer payments is a sin against taxpayers and God, a sin we can no longer afford to commit.

Today in America, our legal system is dominated by a bureaucracy. Our Congress sets new records each year on the amount of legislation it passes, averaging about five hundred new laws a year. The real lawmakers, however, are the bureaucrats, who have no system of checks and balances. Bureaucratic regulations, which affect millions, simply move from the bureaucrats' mouth to the law books. No one votes for these bureaucrats, and no one votes on the confusing and often contradictory rules that they pump out. American citizens are not only saddled with the tyranny of majority via Congress, but also with the tyranny of bureaucracy. No one knows exactly how many laws are on the federal books.

In order for our country to enjoy the freedom and prosperity it once enjoyed, we need a major change in our law base. The law, which we as Christians are obligated to follow, is a hindrance to freedom. A proper biblical law base is one that protects freedom, not one that destroys it. Our laws allow for paper money, confiscatory taxation, and overwhelming regulation. These laws must change before we can expect a brighter economic picture. The essence of government is law. When government goes bad, its laws go bad. As long as we sit passively while the government frantically pumps out more and more complex laws that intrude on free movement in the marketplace, the only changes we can expect to see will be for the worse. While people march on Washington demanding more government redistribution, interference, and intervention, we sit in our easy chairs watching the evening news. We need active inaction with regard to spending programs and action with regard to changing our law base.

The pleas are generally the same: "Write your legislators," "Support a candidate," "Run for office," "Join a committee." These calls come from all sides of the political spectrum and produce few results. We are involved in a war of ideas. The best weapon is not letter-writing or campaigning, but education. Public opinion is a strong force in America today. It is not swayed by political speeches; it is not swayed by burning editorials. Public opinion changes one mind at a time, through private conversations, one to one. Forget Emily Post and discuss politics. Each new convert to the cause of Christian freedom is another soldier in the war of ideas. To be effective, one must be educated—not necessarily with a degree in economics or political science, but with a clear understanding of the way the market works, the effects of government interference, and biblical principles that relate to economics. An educated layman is more effective than ten economic scholars. But the most clear-thinking layperson is totally ineffective if he or she continues to use the government for private gain. Hypocrisy does not help the cause of freedom; education and dedication do.

The first Tuesday following the first Monday of every November is a difficult time for many Christians, for whom voting presents an ethical dilemma. Rarely does a candidate have a platform that is entirely faithful to Scripture. Voting leaves us with three choices. We can vote for one of the two candidates offered. We can use the write-in process, saying no to both official candidates. Or we can not vote at all.

Voting for one candidate amounts to choosing the lesser of two evils. If one vote is an endorsement of the unbiblical graduated income tax, and another vote is an endorsement of abortion, whom do you vote for, or do you vote for neither? Not voting endorses neither, but it still allows one to take office. The dilemma is difficult.

Not voting is one way to demonstrate displeasure with the available candidates. But not voting can easily be attributed to voter apathy rather than to voter anger. We are left with a difficult dilemma, every first Tuesday after the first Monday of November.

Recently there has been much talk and little action concerning budget deficits. Conservatives historically have argued that a balanced budget is a necessity. Finally, in 1980, a conservative was elected president. The president has the responsibility of writing each fiscal year's budget which is then passed on to Congress for approval. The president wrote his first budget, and after much bickering it was approved by Congress. Rather than presenting the American people with the first balanced budget since the Kennedy administration, the president produced a budget with an all-time high deficit. Reagan has repeated this performance every year since then. If the symbol of conservative politics, Ronald Reagan, will not balance the budget, who will? Although many conservative legislators who do not enjoy the position of budget writer have tried to stop this vice of deficit spending, the law requiring all budgets to be balanced has been ignored. The solution suggested by some conservative legislators is to make a law so strong that it cannot be ignored—an amendment to our Constitution.

The adoption of an amendment to the Constitution requiring annually balanced budgets would have a significant effect on the economy. A balanced budget automatically eliminates inflation. The printing of fiat money would instantly cease, freeing more money for saving and therefore for increased capital investment. A balanced budget would dramatically hamper government spending. The government can only tax its citizens so much. Taxation beyond a certain point brings an angry reaction from voters. Politicians have gotten around this problem by paying for their pet programs with inflated dollars. That option is eliminated with a balanced budget amendment. With a political ceiling on tax rates and no inflation, government spending would have to go down, leaving money for production purposes in the marketplace. Passage of such an amendment would alert politicians that the American citizenry is tired of fiscal irresponsibility. It would alert our politicians that we are watching them, and that they must respect our intelligence.

We need to support such an amendment vocally. A grass-roots support system would insure its passage in the near future. The sooner we have such an amendment, the sooner we can begin to build a strong and healthy economy. The importance of a balanced budget cannot be obscured. We must require our government to practice good stewardship, to practice sound "house-rule." We must hold our government and ourselves, those who put these men and women into office, accountable for spending more than we have. The power to inflate is a danger we cannot safely overlook.

A bleak economic future is the only thing any conservative economist can foresee as long as we remain inactive. We must actively work to stop government spending. The battle does not start in the media nor in the voting booths, but at home. Each government check that comes into our homes is a part of the problem. As long as there is a demand for government spending, the government will meet it, at the ultimate expense of the taxpayer. At home we can face the problem, not only by refusing government assistance but also by talking with friends and neighbors. We must educate ourselves and those around us. A small-government mindset in America will produce small government. Ignorance, on the other hand, will allow the government to grow to bigger and more frightening proportions.

The pulpit is an excellent place for education. If our ministers fear to speak out against government growth, they soon may not enjoy the freedom to do so. Holistic preaching demands that we approach the subject of public policy. God found it important enough to include it in Scriptures, and we should be able to find it in our churches. Certainly the subject may cause division, but all truth does.

What can we do? We can learn, we can teach, and we can pray for our leaders. Face the issues and study them in light of the Bible. Prayer and education are the two strongest tools the Christian can use. Use them, and call our nation to discipleship, under God, with liberty and justice for all.

NOTES

1 John Calvin, *Institutes of the Christian Religion*, Vol. 1 (Philadel-
phia: Presbyterian Board of Christian Education, 1932), p. 371.
2 Adam Smith, *An Inquiry Into the Nature and Causes of the Wealth of
Nations* (New York: The Modern Library, 1900), p. 14.
3 Paul Einzig, *Primitive Money* (London: Eyre and Spottiswoode,
1948), p. 198.
4 Garet Garrett, *The People's Pottage* (Caldwell, Idaho: Caxton Print-
ers Ltd., 1965), p. 27.
5 Ibid, p. 32.
6 James Hasting, *Dictionary of the Bible*, Vol. 1 (New York: Charles
Scribners Sons, 1898), p. 629.
7 Yehezkel Kaufmann, *The Religion of Israel* (Chicago: University of
Chicago Press, 1960), pp. 319–20.
8 Karl Barth, *Doctrine of Reconciliation* (Edinburgh: T. & T. Clarke,
1956), p. 18.
9 Gerhard Kittle, *Bible Key Words*, Vol. 1, Book 4 (New York: Harper
and Brothers Publishers, 1951), p. 23.
10 Murray Rothbard, *Man, Economy and State* (Los Angeles: Nash
Publishing Corporation, 1970), p. 818.
11 Ibid, p. 931.
12 Philip Hughes, *Paul's Second Epistle to the Corinthians* (Grand Rapids: Wm. B. Eerdmans Publishing Company, 1962), p. 306.
13 J. B. Lightfoot, *Saint Paul's Epistles to the Colossians and to Phile-
mon* (Grand Rapids: Zondervan, 1959), p. 210.

14 Ronald Nash, *Social Justice and the Christian Church* (Milford, Mich.: Mott Media, 1983), p. 31.
15 Ibid, pp. 28, 29.
16 William Simon, *A Time For Truth* (New York: MacGraw-Hill Book Company, 1978), p. 90.
17 Smith, *Wealth of Nations*, p. 424.